ASL-to-English Interpretation:

Say It Like They Mean It

Jean Elaine Kelly

RID Press
Registry of Interpreters for the Deaf, Inc.
333 Commerce Street
Alexandria, VA 22314   USA
(703) 838-0030 V, (703) 838-0459 TTY
www.rid.org

Registry of Interpreters for the Deaf

RID is a national membership organization representing the professionals who facilitate communication between people who are deaf or hard of hearing and people who can hear. Established in 1964 and incorporated in 1974, RID is a tax-exempt 501(c)(3) nonprofit organization.

It is the mission of RID to provide international, national, regional, state and local forums and an organizational structure for the continued growth and development of the profession of interpretation and transliteration of American Sign Language and English.

RID Press is the professional publishing arm of RID. The mission of RID Press is to extend the reach and reputation of RID through the publication of scholarly, practical, artistic and educational materials that advance the learning and knowledge of the profession of interpreting. The Press seeks to reflect the mission of RID by publishing a wide range of works that promote recognition and respect for the language and culture of deaf people and the practitioners in the field.

RID Press is a division of the Registry of Interpreters for the Deaf, 333 Commerce St, Alexandria, VA 22314, USA, (703) 838-0030, (703) 838-0459 TTY, www.rid.org

Published 2004

Library of Congress Catalog Card Number: 2003092659

ISBN 0-916883-38-8

Printed in the United States of America

Contents

 # Acknowledgments

First and foremost, I want to thank my husband, Ian, for all his support.

Next, it is impossible to mention all those individuals who have, through their ideas and creativity, been an influence to me, but I do wish to thank the following people for taking the time out of their busy schedules to help create this book.

Steve Phan, who encouraged my endeavor with his feedback and support of my work.

Christine Smith, who helped push me to dig deeper than I would have on my own and helped develop my ideas.

Melanie Nakaji, who gave me her feedback from the Deaf consumer's perspective.

My editor, Carol Tipton, who was encouraging and supportive as she helped me with ensuring the information in the book was clear.

My interpreting students, for being willing to let me practice on them.

 # Introduction

3/22/23

Over the years, working as a community and educational interpreter, I have sought, with my colleagues, to find the best way to present an appropriate and clear ASL-to-English interpretation. Together we looked at what was needed to produce an equivalent and accurate interpretation and worked on our capabilities to present the message into appropriate and idiomatic English. The results and findings are the impetus for this text.

When working with interpreting students, I noted the same questions and concerns would come up again and again. The students' questions often dealt with how to interpret what they saw in ASL into English that best presented the message they had seen. Looking at and exploring the different ways to help students understand what was needed in their interpretation is the focus of this text.

While working with English-speaking consumers, there were times when I understood the message, but from my interpretation, the consumer did not. In order to improve my interpretation, I listened to other interpreters and worked on discovering how they would present the English interpretation. To better understand how to interpret to an English-speaking audience is the reason for this text.

The focus of *ASL-to-English Interpretation: Say It Like They Mean It*, is not about how we the interpreters think the English interpretation should be presented, but rather, how would an English-speaking consumer with no understanding of the Deaf culture best understand the voiced message. Interpreting preparation programs across the country help teach their students how to work between two languages. Issues that arise when going between these two languages, one auditory and the other visual, are addressed in this book.

The task of producing an appropriate interpretation from ASL-to-English is often noted as being the more difficult of the two tasks. With only two years in most interpreting preparation programs, students may not have a full comprehension of what is expected in the ASL-to-English interpretation. This book, hopefully, will not only give students an opportunity to learn how to interpret from ASL-to-English, but will also give students the opportunity to discuss the task of the English interpretation with their teacher and fellow students.

The need for good ASL-to-English interpretation is continuing to expand. As Deaf consumers take on positions that require them to be the purveyors and not merely the recipients of information, the work of interpreting ASL-to-English has never been greater. Both Deaf and hearing consumers should expect and receive the best interpretation possible. This book is an attempt to organize and share information out in the field that relates to the work of how best to convey the signed message to a hearing consumer.

This book was written with two goals in mind. The primary goal is to have a standardized curriculum that can be used in interpreter preparation programs. This book should enhance the information already being taught in your program by your teacher. The second goal is to improve the ASL-to-English skills of interpreters who have completed an interpreter preparation program by providing a better understanding of the components needed in the task of ASL-to-English interpretation. As an accumulation of my work, my observations, and other research in the field of interpreting, this book is an evolving process that can only be enhanced by the contributions of others.

Chapter One

ASL-to-English Interpretation: An Overview

"You gave a magnificent speech, but your interpreter was eloquent."
—Charles de Gaulle to Richard Nixon

Why a Book on ASL-to-English Interpretation?

The goal of any Sign-to-English interpretation is to produce an accurate and equivalent message from the source language to the target language that utilizes appropriate vocabulary, conveys the content well, demonstrates proper English structure, and portrays the signer's affect. To do this, interpreters take the signed message of Deaf consumers and produce an English interpretation in order to tell it like they mean it.

The task of sign language interpreting involves either interpreting a message from English to a signed language (Sign) or from Sign-to-English. These two components, which are of equal importance, are sometimes learned or taught as separate tasks. When talking about a Sign-to-English interpretation, the term "voicing" is often used, which may give the impression that the ability to present a message from Sign-to-English is merely a vocalization of the signs used, not a true interpretation. Interpretation does, however, occur in both English-to-Sign and Sign-to-English interpreting. The goal for the interpreter is to take the message conveyed in one language and produce this message in another language so it is clearly rendered and understood by the consumers.

Interpreting into English requires many of the same skills as interpreting into ASL. Yet often when informed an assignment will consist of a Sign-to-English interpretation as the major component of the job, the interpreter will refuse to take it or become apprehensive. One reason for this apprehension is that interpreters have not really analyzed how to make an interpretation sound like native English. English speakers use language in a variety of different ways: when introducing a point, ending a story, telling a joke, or performing the myriad of other tasks that occur naturally in the English language.

Interpreter training programs (ITPs) teach students how to make an interpreted message clear to Deaf consumers, but not as much focus is placed on learning about hearing consumers and their needs. These consumers need a clear interpretation as much as Deaf consumers do, especially if the English speakers are unfamiliar with Deaf culture and the interpreting process. Interpreting students need to learn in their Sign-to-English classes how to make the English interpretation more accurate, e.g., how to make pronoun referents clear, how to use verb tense appropriately, and how to choose words and phrases that sound natural in English.

Often the needs of hearing consumers are overlooked or ignored. As these consumers depend primarily on auditory cues for information, they usually do not clue into the visual-gestural components of ASL and often do not understand Deaf culture. Taking an English speaker's perspective and lack of understanding into account is a necessary component in order to produce a quality interpretation.

Interpreters give "voice" to a Deaf consumer's message. They do not speak their own thoughts; yet they choose to use certain words and phrases and therefore have an impact on the ability of the audience to understand the message intended by the presenter. Dale Carnegie noted, "Every activity of our lives is communication of a sort, but it is through speech that man asserts his distinctiveness, that he best expresses his own individuality, his essence" (Vasalla, 1998, p. 78). Thus the interpreter's job is to portray the signer's essence through effective use of the English language.

The ability to render a Sign-to-English interpretation has always been a key component of national certification performance exams. Any test used for evaluating interpreters involves both an English-to-Sign portion and a Sign-to-English component. An interpreter must pass both segments in order to become certified.

Therefore, this book will explore the components of an effective Sign-to-English interpretation and guide the reader with practical exercises aimed at increasing skill in each area.

The Hearing Consumer

The 1978 RID convention proceedings feature nine articles under the section, "The Consumer." Even though the vast majority of interpreting assignments involve at least one Deaf and one hearing consumer, only one of these articles mentions the English-speaking consumer. Until recently, a review of RID literature would reveal very few articles dealing with hearing consumers. Even the name of the national organization, the Registry of Interpreters for the Deaf, makes reference only to Deaf consumers. Workshops, classes, and articles have traditionally dealt with how interpreters work with Deaf consumers. The needs of hearing consumers have been largely overlooked.

For example, the 1980 RID convention proceedings include an article on Sign-to-English interpreting (Carlson & Morgan). Its focus, while valid and important, is not on English-speaking consumers and the target language they would need, but rather on helping interpreting students get through a Sign-to-English class in an interpreter training program. In the appendix, the authors state ten hints for Sign-to-English interpreting, one of which is to make contact with Deaf consumers. This is necessary, but never are the hearing consumers acknowledged or recognized. Students are not told to pay attention to the language of the hearing consumer; nor are they told to become fully proficient in or familiar with the various means of expression that occur in the English language. It seems as if the field of interpreting has been so focused on ASL and Deaf consumers that the other consumers have been forgotten. Without persons who can hear and who know little or nothing about the Deaf community, its language and its culture, there would be no need for interpreting services.

Frishberg (1990), writing about consumers' comprehension of an interpreter, states, "The important question to ask is how well the deaf viewer will understand the interpreter" (p. 41). This is fine, but interpreters should not neglect the English speaker's comprehension of the message as well. Perhaps the English-speaking consumer is not taken into consideration because it is incorrectly assumed that any interpreter who is a native speaker of English possesses proficiency in the English language. However, interpreting students are largely unaware of how English varies among speakers and situations. Students learn that some Deaf consumers may be oral, others use ASL, while others prefer a more English transliteration. Interpreters also need to consider the following questions about hearing consumers:

Are they native English users?

What is their educational level?

How much knowledge might they have about Deaf culture and the Deaf community?

The answer to each question will affect how an interpreter renders a message into English.

Previous Views of Sign-to-English Interpretation

When the field of sign language interpretation was being defined in 1964 and later recorded in the book *Interpreting for Deaf People*, the task of interpreting from English-to-Sign was called "interpreting," while the task of Sign-to-English interpreting was labeled "reverse interpreting" (Quigley & Youngs, 1965). Interpreting was only referred to as "an explanation of another person's remarks through the language of signs" (p. 6). In 1981, Solow defined interpreting as the "process of transmitting spoken English into American Sign Language and/or gestures for communication between deaf and hearing people" (p. XI), but not the process of transmitting American Sign Language into spoken English.

The New Deaf Consumer

Much has changed in our profession over the years. The need to render a message into English occurs more often now than when the profession was first beginning. Where interpreters once only worked with Deaf students, they now interpret for Deaf teachers and administrators. In the past there were only Deaf employees in the business world, but now there are Deaf supervisors, Deaf group facilitators, and Deaf employers. Whereas previously the Deaf consumer was often only the recipient of information, now he or she is frequently the conveyer of information, and therefore the interpreter's ability to interpret into English is more critical.

Who Defines the Role of Interpreters?

Currently, Deaf consumers, more than hearing consumers, define the role of interpreters. Deaf consumers are much more involved in the education of sign language interpreters than their hearing counterparts. This involvement is noted in the push by the profession for Deaf consumers to either attend or present during interpreting workshops and conferences and to write articles in professional journals and newsletters. Noting that Deaf people are the experts of ASL (Stauffer, 1991), their involvement in the training of interpreters is critical. However, unless hearing persons are somehow involved in the Deaf community, either as interpreters, parents of Deaf children, or relatives of Deaf people, there is not a similar desire for them to be involved.

People with little or no contact with the Deaf community would probably not want to be active participants in defining the role of or discussing the task interpreters do. The hearing population is so large and diverse, it seems an impossible task to get representative involvement from members of the English-speaking community. Currently, there is some involvement as the RID does use English speakers with no knowledge of signing or Deaf culture as raters for national performance examinations. Along with this, hearing consumers are often asked to give feedback to referral agencies about the interpreting services received, but more input is needed.

A Language, B Language ✓

The International Association of Conference Interpreters for spoken languages established language classification standards which deal with a person's A or B language (Seleskovitch, 1978). The A language is the one learned at home, one's native language. It is the language in which one is most fluent, is most capable of discussing a wide variety of topics, and the one in which a person has little trouble deciphering the meaning behind the words. The B language is acquired through classes, through interaction with people who use it, and by formal study. Specific topics and jargon may prove difficult, and some nuances of meaning may be lost to a non-native speaker. Spoken-language interpreters work almost exclusively from their learned language (B language) into their native language (A language) (Humphrey & Alcorn, 1995). A competent spoken language interpreter must have a "total feel for the language so that the expressions he uses will sound immediately familiar to his listeners, leaving them free to concentrate on the content of the message" (Seleskovitch, 1978, p. 74).

Humphrey (1995, p. 155) writes, "Some people contend that sign-to-voice interpreting is the harder part of the process since reading signs is more challenging than producing signs. This is a common misperception. Actually, if one's second language is acquired in an appropriate manner, s/he should be much stronger working from her/his second language into her/his native language."

Frishberg (1990) states that "the practice among sign language interpreters is to interpret into one's B language from one's A language" (p. 16), and later states that there are only some situations that require going into the interpreter's A language, English. This is in contrast to spoken language interpreters, who work mostly into their native language while listening to the message in their second language (Lawrence, 1994). However, with more Deaf professionals in the field today, the need for sign language interpreters to interpret into their A language has dramatically increased.

Challenges of Sign-to-English Interpreting

Expressive

Many sign language interpreters say that they prefer working from English to ASL. Some interpreters state that comprehending ASL is more difficult than producing ASL. Most likely it is not the comprehension of the individual signs that proves difficult, but rather the tendency to try to follow the syntax of ASL while producing an English interpretation. The message found in ASL is dependent not merely on the signs, but also on prosodic features such as the use of space, rhythm, and visual cues working together to convey meaning. English, an auditory-oral language, is also not dependent solely on words, but uses tone, pacing, and sound to convey meaning. Part of the challenge of interpreting ASL into English is to include not only the information found in the signs, but to also include the meaning conveyed by non-manual markers.

In addition, Tipton (1999) notes that Sign-to-English interpreters do face some unique challenges:

Visual Acuity

- First, receiving a visual message requires more effort than listening to information presented in spoken form. The eyes use voluntary muscles which must physically locate a signer and remain focused on the message, whereas the ears are part of the autonomic nervous system and, as such, do not feel fatigued, cannot be turned off and on, and receive information with no effort.

- Second, because Sign uses space, a Sign-to-English interpreter must take this 3-dimensional message and render it into a 1-dimensional message. "A picture is worth a thousand words" may be almost literally true when interpreting a signed description of spatial information into spoken English.

Time, Mood, Pronouns

- Third, ASL is not usually taught to native users in school and has no standard written form. The language also allows for new signs to be invented by individual users. Some Deaf people may use ASL as their primary mode of communication, but not all deaf people are fluent in ASL (Kannapell, 1982, 1989). Many Deaf people are bilingual in English and ASL, in varying degrees. The source language used by Deaf consumers may consist of a little bit of English and a little bit of ASL. Rarely is it a "pure" delivery of either language. The tendency for signed discourse to be a blended form of ASL and English syntax may be an outcome of a

Clarification = trust

bilingual community (Bragg, 1990). Therefore much more variation occurs in sign communication than spoken English discourse. Even with advance preparation, interpreters will more likely than not see unfamiliar signs than to hear unfamiliar words.

- Fourth, when hearing an unfamiliar term, name or foreign word, English-to-Sign interpreters, if they cannot interrupt the speaker and ask for clarification, can either mouth the word, and/or attempt to fingerspell it phonetically. Conversely, when Sign-to-English interpreters observe an unfamiliar sign, they have no recourse but to interrupt the speaker if the meaning cannot be ascertained through context.

- Fifth, a hearing audience is probably less forgiving of interpreter errors than a deaf audience, which more often has familiarity with the interpreting process, knows that Sign varies from person to person, and may even know the interpreter personally.

Of course, Deaf presenters are also very concerned that their message be delivered clearly. A common complaint Deaf people have is that "most hearing interpreters possess poor voicing skills, so the Deaf person ends up sounding idiotic or unintelligible" (Baker-Shenk, 1991, p. 122). Baker-Shenk also goes on to say that interpreters maintain a power imbalance "when the interpreter poorly voices for the Deaf person but hides that fact from the hearing people as well as the Deaf person" (1991, p. 125). If the target language, English, is unclear or incoherent to the consumers listening, they are unable to distinguish whether the interpreter or the Deaf person is making the errors.

Components of a Sign-to-English Interpretation

A basic and very general model of the process of communication is Berlo's Source, Message, Channel, Receiver (SMCR) model (1960):

Source made up of:	Message made up of:	Channel through:	Receiver made up of:
Communication skills Attitudes Knowledge Social system Culture	Structure Content Code	Seeing Hearing Touching Smelling Tasting	Communication skills Attitudes Knowledge Social system Culture

The source is the speaker, and the receiver is the listener. Both are dependent on the same attributes, which include attitude and culture found in the message, not merely the words that comprise the communication process. Interpreting adds one more component to this model.

The Conference of Interpreter Trainers (1984), analyzed the task of interpretation, and then defined what was needed to understand the source message before an interpretation could be rendered. The components of understanding require the interpreter to:

1. Decode and decipher the message, to know the meaning of the signs or words being used.
2. Think.
3. Anticipate and predict, by linking pre-existing knowledge with current content.
4. Process information and assess how to interpret it.

5. Remember what was said (short-term memory) and refer back to pre-existing knowledge (long-term memory).

6. Attend to and concentrate on the message.

Another model comes from Colonomos (1989). It is composed of the interpreter:

1. Taking in information received from the source language.

2. Analyzing the message conveyed by the source language.

3. Constructing meaning from the information received.

4. Analyzing how to portray an equivalent message in the target language.

5. Producing the message into the target language.

In 1995 the RSA Federal Interpreting Center developed a *Curriculum for Training Interpreters for the Deaf in Educational and Rehabilitation Settings*, which identifies and defines the following key elements necessary for an effective Sign-to-English interpretation (p. 14):

1. Vocabulary selection. The interpreter must choose appropriate English words, showing a variety in the vocabulary selection, avoiding repetition.

2. Message conveyed. The content should be accurately conveyed and rendered faithfully. There should be no skewing of the message or conceptual errors in stating the message.

3. English structure. The interpreter must adhere to the rules of grammar, effectively expressing the signed message into proper English, using an appropriate selection of pronouns, verb tenses, and modifiers.

4. Signer affect conveyed. The interpreter must understand the presenter's perspective and convey the speaker's emotions, mood and style of speaking.

Summary

The area of Sign-to-English interpretation has been viewed quite differently than English-to-Sign interpretation throughout the history of sign language interpretation. When the field began in 1964, Sign-to-English interpretation was referred to as "reverse interpreting." Later, this task has been referred to as "voice interpreting." As consumers have changed, the need for Sign-to-English interpreting has increased dramatically.

Throughout the growth of the profession, Deaf consumers have traditionally had input into defining the role of interpreters. Deaf consumers are involved in teaching workshops, attending conferences, and writing papers in professional journals. Hearing consumers are often overlooked in defining this role.

Spoken language interpreters generally interpret from their B language into their A language. In the field of ASL/English interpreting, however, most of the work has traditionally been done from the A language into the B language, but this is changing. Sign-to-English interpreting contains some unique challenges: using the eyes instead of the ears to receive the message, rendering a three-dimensional message into one dimension, experiencing a great amount of variation in the source message, and dealing with consumers who are relatively unfamiliar with the interpreting process.

The basic components of Sign-to-English interpretation are the same as English-to-Sign interpretation. The interpreter:

- Takes in information from the source language.

- Conducts an analysis of the message conveyed.

- Constructs the meaning from the information received.

- Analyzes how to portray the information in the target language.

- Produces the message in the target language.

When interpreting into English, four key components to be aware of are vocabulary selection, message conveyed, English structure, and signer affect conveyed.

Activity 1-1

Discussion and group work

Step 1:   Form small groups of 4-6 people.

Step 2:   Discuss the following questions and write down the answers:

Before working on an English-to-ASL interpretation, what skills should an interpreter possess?

Before working on an ASL-to-English interpretation, what skills should an interpreter possess?

What are the similarities and differences between the two lists?

What can interpreters do to increase their English vocabulary?

State one activity or class you would like to take to improve English vocabulary or speaking skills.

Step 3:   Come back together as a class and discuss the answers.

Activity 1-2

Creating a baseline for progress

At the beginning of the class each student should make an audiotape recording of an ASL-to-English interpretation to establish a baseline.

Students should try to interpret into English using complete sentences, adequate volume, tone, and expression. They should try to incorporate appropriate word choices and English grammar, paying special attention to the handling of direct address, pronouns, spatial information, classifiers, topic/comment, and reading of fingerspelling and numbers.

Students should not review the tape, but keep it in a location where it can be found at the end of class, to re-record.

At the end of the class, using the same material, the student will re-record him/herself interpreting the same material into English. There is an exercise in Chapter 10 that will ask the student questions about the interpretation. By reviewing both audiotapes, the student will be able to note his or her progress.

Chapter Two

The Other Consumer

I had just graduated from my ITP, and I needed to call one of my Deaf teachers to get a reference. Not having a TTY yet, I had to use the relay. I needed a reference because there was a great opportunity with a project at NTID, co-sponsored by Gallaudet, to be a voice-interpreter mentee, and I wanted that opportunity. After that, I planned to be involved in a mentorship with a Deaf agency.

- An interpreter reading the paragraph above could probably understand everything that was written, including all of its ramifications and implications. However, suppose it was a favorite, older aunt reading the paragraph. She would most likely not be familiar with certain words and acronyms used and would, therefore, miss most of the message. An average English-speaking person who has not had much or any contact with the Deaf community is not familiar with the terms or jargon used in the Deaf community and the interpreting profession.

The Influence of Culture

- The language a person uses is embedded within the culture in which the person lives. Understanding spoken or written communication is dependent on prior contextual experiences. When someone has not had any experience with a particular language and then uses an interpreter, it becomes the responsibility of the interpreter to provide an interpretation that allows the recipient to infer what is intended from the source (Metzger, 1999). Working between cultures is one of the most difficult aspects of interpreting. People in any culture tend to look at things from their own perspective. Many of the words which appear to be equivalent in two languages are not (Larson, 1998). For example, the Spanish word "galera," besides meaning "gallery," can also mean a "women's jail" or "tall hat."

- Whenever interpreting occurs, there are at least two consumers, each with a unique culture, language, and identity. Interpreting into English does not only entail the work of going from one language to another, but also involves interpreting from one culture to another. Every person is strongly influenced by his or her own culture, and for that reason the ideas, behaviors, and beliefs held by that person are seen as "the right way" (Brislin, 1981). Therefore, he or she will often try to superimpose his or her own values, beliefs, and behaviors on people encountered from other cultures.

Culture can be viewed in three different ways (Gish, 1991):

- **Ethnocentrism**—the attitude that one's culture is superior to others, and that one's beliefs, values, and behaviors are more correct.

- **Xenocentrism**—the belief that anything foreign is best, and one's own lifestyle, products, or ideas are inferior to others.

- **Cultural relativism**—behaviors, lifestyles, and ideas of a certain culture are judged within their own context rather than by the standards of another culture. This is the approach taken by anthropologists.

- People who are not exposed to and who do not study other cultures will probably be ethnocentric. Interpreters, then, must make any necessary cultural adjustments for those who are not familiar with or who have not yet been exposed to Deaf culture. As interpreting students lose their own ethnocentrism, their ability to interpret for consumers from varying cultural backgrounds will be enhanced.

Interpreters strive for equivalency between two languages and two cultures. Merely encoding words (the lexical items), taking the grammatical structures of the source language and producing equivalent lexical items and grammatical structures of the target language, is not enough (Zimmer, 1991). People need to understand each other. This understanding is accomplished not only by having a common language, but also by having an agreed-upon concept of what the words represent (Schein, 1992).

Therefore, interpreters must make sure that culturally implicit information in the source language will be explicit in the target language. Each language labels particular areas of reality or experience differently. Therefore, a hearing person may not understand what a Deaf person really means by the use of certain words.

Culture Influences Meaning

- Cokely (2001) dealt with the issue of what hearing people knew about the terminology used by Deaf people in his article "Interpreting Culturally Rich Realities: Research Implications for Successful Interpretations." In a study conducted in 1999, he interviewed 190 English speakers about their knowledge and understanding of eight English words commonly used in Deaf culture: "mainstreaming," "cochlear implant," "sign language," "ASL," "Gallaudet," "hearing," "hard-of-hearing," and "deaf." The results showed that the meaning Deaf people placed on these words differed significantly from the meaning understood by English speakers. For example, most English speakers still see the word "Deaf" from a pathological perspective instead of a cultural one. Cokely states to interpreters:

  - It is incumbent upon us to remember that our responsibility is first and foremost to convey the meaning and intention of speakers and signers and their texts. In rendering our interpretations, however, we cannot and must not assume that because we have acquired additional semantic senses for lexical items, those for whom we interpret have also acquired those additional semantic senses (p. 39).

These lexical items that interpreters and ASL users are familiar with may need cultural mediation in order to give an equivalent meaning in the English interpretation. The idea of cultural mediation is not unique to sign language interpreters. A Spanish interpreter once told of her experience when she was listening to a Cuban interpreter. When someone mentioned a particular date, the Cuban interpreter added, "the day of the glorious revolution," as this is the day that Castro took control of Cuba. The date alone would mean nothing to anyone unfamiliar with Cuban culture and its history. The Cuban interpreter added this information to signify the importance of the date to that culture.

Spingarn (2001) also looked at how words are perceived differently in Deaf and hearing cultures. Her study dealt with an English speaker's knowledge of the Deaf community and its related terms and symbols. The following 15 words/acronyms/symbols were shown to 20 English-speaking respondents:

(handwritten, vertical left margin: Implicit→Explicit)

TTY *Teletype*	TTY (symbol) *(Phone)(Typewriter)*
ADA *American Disability Act*	Mainstream education
Interpreter	Interpreter (symbol) *(ASL Sign)*
Deaf	Ear (symbol) *Assistive Listening Device*
NAD *National Association of the Deaf*	American Sign Language
ASL	Gallaudet University
Closed Captioned	Closed captioned (symbol) *CC*
Relay Operator	

Out of a possible 300 responses, 134 were answered correctly, 128 were incorrect, and 38 were ambiguous. The results of this study show that words and symbols which sign language interpreters are familiar with are probably not familiar to the average English speaker. The study concluded:

> that most people do not possess a broad enough understanding of even the most basic Deaf community-related terminology to be able to adequately navigate a communication situation with a Deaf person without an interpreter present to provide adequate and appropriate lexical-level explanations and cultural mediation (p. 76).

Often when people learn new information, they assume others know it too. These two studies clearly demonstrate that as interpreting students learn new information about a culture and language different from their own, they must keep in mind that most English speakers have not learned this same information. Cokely (2001) concludes his study with the statement that interpreters must be ever mindful of the "ignorance of the other." Interpreters need to be aware of this lack of knowledge during an English interpretation and give English speakers additional information in order to help them fully understand what a Deaf participant is saying. They can do this by saying what each letter in an acronym represents or by adding cultural information that would clarify the interpretation.

Implications for the Interpretation

Many interpreters are unsure of how to best supplement an English interpretation with necessary cultural information without adding too much. The needs of hearing consumers are no different than those of Deaf consumers in this regard. In workshops and classrooms interpreters are taught that when interpreting from English to ASL, they need to drop form and look for meaning, seek language equivalency, or simply explain to the Deaf consumer what is meant by what was said. In *Interpreting for Deaf People* (1965), the authors state, "for many deaf people, it is necessary to paraphrase, define, and explain a speaker's words in terms and concepts which they can understand" (p. 1). For consumers who can hear, it may also be necessary to paraphrase, define, and explain a speaker's signs in ways English-speaking consumers can understand.

Even though the signer is giving the speech, the interpreter is the one who needs to effectively deliver the message in such a way that the English-speaking audience will receive it clearly. Any time a speech is given, an analysis of the audience is helpful (Vassallo, 1990). Information about audience members, that would prove helpful to the interpreter could include:

- Age

- Educational background and level of sophistication

- Occupations represented

- Prior knowledge about the Deaf community
- Ethnicity

Knowing information about the audience will help the interpreter choose appropriate words, use any special jargon applicable to the group, and decide whether or not there needs to be any cultural adjustments, major or minor.

English Language Differences

Interpreters cannot assume that all speakers of English have the same ability to understand what is being said. For example, they may have learned English as a second language, or perhaps they are a group of senior citizens taking an evening class from a Deaf representative from the telephone company, learning about equipment provided to help them as they become hard-of-hearing. Or the consumers may be 18- to 22-year-old students taking a Deaf culture class from a Deaf instructor to satisfy social science requirements for a college degree. In all three cases, the language and experience of the hearing consumers will have to be taken into consideration, along with the other factors listed above in order for the interpretation to be effective.

Solow (1981) states that "hearing audiences, being generally less exposed to interpreters, rely differently on the interpreter than the average deaf audience." Because English-speaking consumers may never have encountered interpreters before, they are not used to making internal adjustments or modifications to the interpretation that they hear. These hearing consumers may also attribute an inarticulate interpretation to a Deaf presenter's incompetence instead of interpreter error. For these reasons, the interpreter must be sure that the interpretation is clear and accurate. To develop Sign-to-English skills, interpreters need to spend a great deal of time associating with the Deaf community to learn to read and understand signs, but this is not enough. Students also need to associate with English speakers who possess a good command of English. Students should note the different ways English words are put together to convey meaning.

Solow cautions interpreters not to "add information to the spoken portion that is not expressed in the signed portion" (p. 55). This warning, though, does not take away from the freedom the interpreter enjoys to make needed cultural and linguistic modifications between the two languages. Interpreters need to incorporate these clarifications or differing lexical choices into their work to ensure an equivalent interpretation for the English-speaking consumer.

One example is the sign INSTITUTE/INSTITUTION. For many Deaf people who have attended a school for the Deaf, this word may evoke memories of a time when they were not the odd man out, but rather, the norm. The English speaker has a different idea of what the word INSTITUTE/INSTITUTION means and may better understand the phrase "residential school for the Deaf," which would not carry a negative connotation. In the same manner, the concept of a HEARING CLASSROOM may be better understood when stated as "a regular classroom with hearing students."

Evaluating the Need for Cultural Adjustments

There may be a need for cultural adjustments during the interpreting process, but these adjustments will not be necessary in every situation. Anna Mindess (2000) offers a list of parameters to consider when deciding whether to make cultural adjustments or not. The first parameter is whether there is parallelism between the cultures. If the content being interpreted is the same in both cultures, there is no need for cultural adjustment.

Second, the interpreter must consider whether the Deaf client identifies with Deaf culture or hearing culture. The use of signs does not always mean that the person identifies with Deaf culture. If the Deaf client identifies more with hearing culture, there may be less of a need for a cultural adjustment in the English interpretation. This may often apply to people who were late deafened.

Next, the people involved may have a high degree of biculturalism. Some Deaf people move comfortably between the two cultures and are aware of hearing norms in many situations. Also, the English-speaking person may have some signing skills or have been exposed to Deaf culture professionally, socially, or personally, and may, therefore, be knowledgeable of Deaf culture and understand the vocabulary and all its implications in Deaf culture.

Finally, the interpreter may be new to a situation where there is an ongoing relationship between the two consumers. These two people may have worked together and have figured out ways of communicating without an interpreter. "If an interpreter makes so many cultural adjustments that the Deaf person seems to have a whole new personality, the hearing consumers may be puzzled" (Mindess, p. 156). In this case, no adjustment would be needed.

Summary

Beginning students of sign language generally do not know much about Deaf culture. Many students feel initially that sign language is based on English. They have no idea of the grammatical, linguistic, or cultural issues they will encounter. Eventually they will learn that American Sign Language is a language in its own right. As they move forward to interpreting, they will see the need to make linguistic and cultural adjustments during the interpreting process.

Classes, workshops, and discussion groups are often geared toward helping interpreters learn how to make linguistic and cultural adjustments during English-to-Sign interpreting. Interpreting assignments generally consist of at least two consumers, one who is Deaf and uses ASL or a signed language and another who can hear and uses English. Both consumers have a language and a culture unique to themselves, and the English-speaking consumer will often need cultural or linguistic adjustments, or explanations of terms used by the Deaf consumer.

Cokely (2001) and Spingarn (2001) each did a study on the recognition of words familiar to Deaf people and interpreters by hearing, English-speaking individuals. Cokely concluded that interpreters need to convey the meaning and the intention of the Deaf consumer to English speakers who do not share the same perspective. Spingarn's study concluded that interpreters need to be aware of the same issues and give English speakers sufficient information in the English interpretation to help them understand what is being said.

Providing an adequate and equivalent English interpretation to hearing consumers requires that interpreters study English usage, American culture, and language variations based on age and geography. Interpreters must think of hearing consumers not as one homogeneous group, but as individuals who need adjustments to the cultural and linguistic information interpreted to them. The interpreter must understand that making certain vocabulary choices for hearing consumers is critical as they have had less experience working with interpreters and rely differently on interpreters than Deaf consumers do.

Activity 2-1

Discussion and group work

Look at the following items. In pairs, come up with a quick way to enhance an English interpretation and express the meaning to someone unfamiliar with Deaf culture.

Example: TTY-TDD, a telecommunication device for the Deaf

NTID

ASL

NAD

PSE

Relay Service

RID

Hearing school

Sim-com

Mainstreaming

CI or CT

CODA

Transliterator

Institute

CIT

Activity 2-2

Given the following information, list factors important to consider during an interpretation into English.

Example: An outreach specialist from a Deaf agency is presenting information to a senior citizens' group about services available to them through the phone company.

Factors to consider:

Age—older.

Awareness—know very little about Deaf culture.

Vocabulary—are not aware of current vocabulary used in the Deaf community.

Other factors—may be hard-of-hearing; thinking process may be slower. The interpreter needs to make points loudly and clearly.

1. A Deaf woman, who has a daughter in the class, is telling a story to a class of second graders. All students can hear.

    Age:

    Awareness:

    Vocabulary:

    Other factors:

2. The Deaf director from a local agency is asking for a donation from a Kiwanis club.

    Age:

    Awareness:

    Vocabulary:

    Other factors:

3. A Deaf linguist is presenting her work at a monthly staff meeting with other linguists from the building.

    Age:

    Awareness:

    Vocabulary:

    Other factors:

4. A Deaf high school student will be presenting a speech for his public speaking class.

    Age:

    Awareness:

    Vocabulary:

    Other factors:

5. A Deaf peer counselor is meeting with a local HIV support group to explain services the agency can offer to Deaf clients.

    Age:

    Awareness:

    Vocabulary:

    Other factors:

6. A Deaf director is making his monthly report to the Board of Directors, which includes both Deaf and hearing members. Some of the hearing members do not sign.

    Age:

    Awareness:

    Vocabulary:

    Other factors:

7. A Deaf woman is applying for a job at a medical warehouse. The interviewer knows no sign language, but has hired two other Deaf individuals this past year.

    Age:

    Awareness:

    Vocabulary:

    Other factors:

Activity 2-3

Discussion and group work

Step 1: In pairs, watch a videotape of a Deaf person signing. Pick out a 2- to 3-minute segment to interpret. Have one person interpret, while the partner takes notes.

Interpret for a child in second grade.

Interpret for a college student.

Interpret for a senior citizen.

Interpret for a person who has only recently learned English.

Step 2: After the person has completed the ASL-to-English interpretation, the partner will share the following information:

What word choices were different or the same in the above scenarios?

Was there more explanation needed for any particular group?

Was there a need to expand or add additional information for a specific group?

How did the form of the interpretation vary for each audience?

Were interpreted sentences in the different scenarios the same length, longer, or shorter? Which ones were different, and why?

Which selection seemed to cause the most difficulty, and why?

Chapter Three

Literal vs. Idiomatic Interpretation

Successful interpretations do not consist of providing one word per sign but, instead, must be in a form that sounds natural to English-speaking consumers. Interpreter training programs often overlook the study and refining of students' first language, English (Patrie, 2000). The idea of working on English skills is often viewed as, "if I can read, write, and speak in my native language, then I should put more study into my second language." Interpreters need to understand the workings of English and have an extensive and competent command of its usage in a variety of situations. The Conference of Interpreter Trainers (1995) states in its National Interpreter Education Standards that the prerequisites for students, after their knowledge of American Sign Language, should include "proficiency in English that at least enables them to converse in a culturally appropriate and participatory fashion, to narrate, and to describe with connected discourse" (p. 9).

Without a strong base of English competency, interpreters may have an idea of a concept that is being presented in ASL, but will be unable to produce an equivalent message into English.

Form and Meaning

- There are two kinds of interpretations; form-based and meaning-based (Larson, 1998). Knowing a word entails being aware of both its form and meaning (Fromkin & Rodman, 1978). The term "form" refers to the words, phrases, clauses, and sentences used in a given language, along with the pronunciation of the words. It is the surface structure, the way the words are arranged. (Larson, 1998). Interpreters must also know the specific agreed-upon meaning of words among the people for whom they are interpreting. They cannot be like Humpty Dumpty from *Through the Looking Glass* who arbitrarily decides meaning when he says:

  "There's glory for you?"

  "I don't know what you mean by 'glory,'" Alice said.

  Humpty Dumpty smiled contemptuously. "Of course you don't—till I tell you. I meant 'there's a nice knock-down argument for you!' "

  "But 'glory' doesn't mean 'a nice knock-down argument.' " Alice objected.

  "When I use a word," Humpty Dumpty said, in rather a scornful tone, "it means just what I choose it to mean—neither more nor less."

  "The question is," said Alice, "whether you can make words mean so many different things."

The meaning from the source language must be held constant as it is presented into the target language. The form will change between languages, but the meaning cannot. Take the following sentences:

> I have a brown dog and a black dog.
> I have two dogs; one is brown, the other is black.

Even though each sentence has its own form, both convey the same meaning.

Levels of Interpretation

While interpreting, a message is changed from the form found in the source language to the form desired in the target language. As information is signed/spoken in one language, the interpreter attempts to convey the information into another language so the recipient of the interpreted message will understand what the speaker intends. The stronger the English competency of the interpreter and his or her ability to work within the constraints of English, the better the output of desired meaning will be in the English interpretation. There are different levels of interpretation: literal, modified literal, idiomatic, and unduly free (Larson, 1995).

Literal

A word-for-word interpretation is called a literal interpretation (Larsen, 1998). Whatever is said in the source language is brought over practically verbatim into the target language. This type of interpretation is unnatural and hard to understand.

A literal interpretation is one in which an English gloss of each sign is spoken.

ASL—MY NAME #P-A-M LAST NAME #C-O-S-T-N-E-R

The literal interpretation would be, "My name is Pam, last name, Costner."

The person listening to that interpretation might understand what is being said, but the sentence itself would not sound normal or natural because it is a form-based interpretation. Another example follows:

ASL—I EARN 10 CEU FOR WORKSHOP

English—I earned 10 CEU for the workshop.

In ASL, the plural is formed when the person signs "10," but in English, adding an "s" to the noun forms the plural. If the interpreter follows the fingerspelled word exactly, the meaning will not be totally lost to the listener, but the sentence will not sound natural.

At times, a literal interpretation makes no sense in English.

ASL—LOOK-APPEARANCE STRONG FATHER

The literal interpretation of "look strong father" has no meaning to an English speaker, or the person may have a completely different impression than what the signer actually meant. The person listening might think the sentence means the person's father looks strong, not the meaning "like the person's father."

A literal interpretation of signs allows for the addition of the verb "to be" or the articles "the" or "a," but it mostly follows the order of the signs. The English words represent signs with one word equaling one sign. This type of interpretation should not be used except in rare instances in which it is asked for, such as in an ASL linguistics class.

There are English-based signing systems, referred to as Manually Coded English (MCE), which were developed to show English in a manual form. These manual codes attempt to reflect the structure and vocabulary of English and should not be confused with a natural signed language (Baker-Shenk, 1987). These sign systems include the Rochester method, Seeing Essential English (SEE1), and Signing Exact English (SEE2) (Humphrey & Alcorn, 1995).

If a Deaf presenter is using one of these codes, the interpretation into spoken English, known as transliteration, will naturally be much more literal, or connected directly to the signs used, than if ASL is used. However, there will usually still need to be some modifications and adjustments to the interpretation to make it sound natural in English. If the Deaf person signs in English order while mouthing English words, the interpretation into spoken English might be almost verbatim, with few modifications between the signed message and the English interpretation.

Modified Literal

The grammar of the source message is modified to use acceptable sentence structure in the target language, but the lexical items are interpreted more literally. For the ASL sentence,

```
HEARING DOG, HAVE
```

the modified literal interpretation would change the sentence structure to "I have a hearing dog." With a modified literal interpretation, the English speakers do not have a clear understanding of what this means. They might think the Deaf person is merely stating that the dog can hear, when in fact, Hearing Dogs are those that have been especially trained to alert their owners to various sounds.

Idiomatic

- This type of interpretation uses natural forms found in the target language and is not dependent on the form of the source language. Grammatical presentation and choice of lexical items are meaning based, not form-based.

- The way a native speaker presents the language is considered idiomatic; it incorporates a speech form that is natural and specific to the language. Spoken English is often presented in a more idiomatic way than written English (Vassallo, 1990). When interpreting from ASL-to-English, the goal is to provide an idiomatic interpretation. Idiomatic speech does include idioms, which are defined in the dictionary as "speech forms that are peculiar to themselves within the usage of a given language," but should not be confused with consisting only of idioms. Idioms include expressions such as, "It's raining cats and dogs" or "I'm going to knock your lights out." Idiomatic speech, however, is characterized by a specialized vocabulary used by a group of people. It consists of expressing ideas using natural forms and jargon. For example, in idiomatic English, one would say, "a bunch of grapes" rather than "a group of grapes," and "He had a black eye" rather than "He had an eye that was bruised."

An English speaker expects to hear certain phrases being said in specific ways. The American flag is red, white, and blue; not blue, red, and white. Both phrases contain the correct information, but when presenting the colors in an order that is not idiomatic, the sentence sounds unnatural to the listener.

In the fairy tale "The Three Little Pigs," the antagonist is the "big, bad wolf," not the "huge, evil wolf." Later he doesn't "blow and blow" until the house falls down. The "big, bad wolf" has to "huff and puff" to "blow the house down." That is the way English speakers expect to hear the story. Look again at the example used in the literal level.

```
MY NAME #P-A-M LAST NAME #C-O-S-T-N-E-R
```

If, instead of a literal interpretation, the interpreter looks for the meaning behind the signs, the form produced would need to sound natural and be easily understood by the English speaker. This would be a meaning-based interpretation. Such an interpretation of the sentence above would be, "My name is Pam Costner" or "I'm Pam Costner."

When combining two words into a phrase, the meaning of each separately sometimes is different than when they are together. For example, the expression, "pig-headed." has nothing to do with the animal, pig, or the head, but means that the person is stubborn. Someone can "fall in love," but not "fall in hate." Someone could say, "It cost me an arm and a leg," but not a "finger and a toe."

A young woman from Germany, with English as her second language, demonstrated this when she wanted to compliment a friend about how active she was, and called her a busybody. When her friend became upset with this compliment, the German woman explained she had used the term because her friend always seemed to be doing something, and therefore was "busy." Imagine her embarrassment when she was told that a busybody, to native English speakers, meant someone that was nosy and getting into other people's business.

Look at the following example of ASL discourse:

I GO-TO VISIT MY MOTHER-FATHER LAST-WEEK WEDNESDAY. MY FATHER HIS BIRTHDAY

An idiomatic interpretation would be, "Last Wednesday, I went to my parents for my father's birthday." Since there is not a one-to-one correlation between signs and words in an idiomatic interpretation, the interpreter keeps the concept intact without speaking one word for each sign. In another example, while interpreting a meeting on the ADA and transportation, a Deaf person might present an issue as follows:

PROBLEM, I GO TROLLEY, WAIT, HEARING PEOPLE HEAR W-H-I-S-T-L-E (Index Plural) CAN, I KNOW-NOTHING UNTIL SEE T-R-O-L-L-E-Y, SAFE NOT, I WANT LIGHT WARN-ME.

A more literal interpretation might be, "One problem is I go to the trolley and wait. The hearing people hear the whistle; they can do that. I know nothing until I see the trolley. This is not safe. I want a light to warn me."

A more idiomatic presentation of the English interpretation might be, "*One issue* for Deaf people is at *trolley stations*. Deaf people can't hear the trolley whistles that warn the other passengers. This could be dangerous, and I would like a warning light installed."

A literal and idiomatic interpretation might convey the same meaning, but the form of the idiomatic interpretation is more natural to English and does not follow the grammatical structure of ASL. The two italicized phrases above make the message sound more idiomatic. English speakers do not have "problems" at business meetings, but "issues," and English speakers may refer to it not as "the trolley" but "the trolley station" to clarify it is the platform itself to which person is referring. Interpreters would need to listen to other English speakers at the meeting in order to recognize how to best present similar information. There may be times when the form of the signed message will have little if any relationship to that of the interpreted message. During a meeting, one Deaf individual made a presentation and at the end signed,

IF YOU HELP US, THEN WE HELP YOU.

The interpreter could have followed the words the Deaf person used, but felt the meaning was better conveyed by "If you scratch our backs, then we'll scratch yours." The meaning was preserved in this idiomatic interpretation. Since speakers of English enjoy plays on words, however, an interpreter needs to be prepared for a response in kind, such as, "Some people have scratchier backs than others!" Since this type of response occurs only rarely, interpreters should not be wary of rendering a message in an idiomatic form.

Unduly Free

This occurs when extraneous information not found in the source message is added to the interpretation which changes the meaning to either have a stronger or weaker impact than that given. A deaf person might sign:

I GRADUATE GALLAUDET

An unduly free interpretation might be, "I graduated from Gallaudet University, *a 4-year university for Deaf people, which allowed me to be part of my own culture and freed me of oppression from hearing people.*" The italicized portion is extraneous information that the interpreter added; it was not present in the source message. Or perhaps a Deaf person telling about his past school experiences, signs:

ME DEAF, BUT GO-TO MAINSTREAM SCHOOL WITH HEARING PEOPLE.

If the interpreter wanted to make this sound cute and interpret it as, "I am a Deafie, but I went to a school with Hearies," this would also be unduly free and not acceptable. Because unduly free interpretations distort the original source message, they should be avoided.

Information Processing

The ability to interpret into idiomatic English depends largely on how an interpreter processes the source material. Interpreters can process information on four levels: lexical, phrasal, sentential, and textual (Colonomos, 1989). These levels vary from a word-by-word treatment to focusing on the entire text.

- **Lexical level**: The interpreter processes one word at a time. There is little if any dropping of form. The resulting interpretation is often very literal and stilted.

- **Phrasal level**: The interpreter stays a phrase behind the speaker. Each phrase is processed as a unit of meaning. For example, "I ran into Jim" contains the phrase, "ran into." These two words together don't mean that I physically ran into Jim, but I "met" Jim or "saw" Jim. Another example is, "the baby fell asleep." The baby does not actually "fall." Rather, the word "fall" goes with "asleep" to make one concept. The resulting interpretation is more idiomatic but still somewhat stilted.

- **Sentential level**: The interpreter processes an entire sentence before interpreting it. The resulting interpretation consists of receiving complete thoughts and interpreting complete thoughts into idiomatic language. The source and target language may be grammatically very different.

- **Textual level**: The interpreter processes multiple sentences to extract meaning. The source language form is dropped effectively. The resulting interpretation is very idiomatic.

For spoken language interpreters, a relationship exists between processing time and the number of errors in the interpreted output (Barik, 1975). With longer processing time, fewer errors occur, resulting in a more accurate and idiomatic interpretation. When examining the work of ASL-to-English interpreters, it has been found that the quality of the output is likewise influenced by the length of processing time (Cokely, 1992). The more information the interpreter waits to receive, the better the interpretation. The interpretation will also be enhanced if the interpreter is aware of the speaker's goal, objectives, and intent. When this awareness is present, the interpreter can think beyond the words and phrases and demonstrate a clear relationship between sentences, paragraphs, and larger chunks of discourse.

Sounding Natural

When moving into unfamiliar material or higher levels of syntactic structure with complex sentences and discourse, there is a tendency for English word choices to be unduly influenced by the lexical items and grammatical forms of the source language, ASL. Syntactic structure refers to the rules of a language in forming sentences, either signed or spoken. Discourse is the language itself, whether it be written, spoken, or signed. Lexical items are the words or signs that make up a language. Grammatical forms are the rules, the signs or words, the sounds, and the basic units of meaning found in a language. For example, the ASL sentence,

```
YES, HAVE TWO HOBBY. P-O-T-T-E-R-Y PAINT. REQUIRE ROOM HAVE MANY WINDOW.
```

can be interpreted as follows:

"Yes, I have two hobbies, pottery and painting. So I would need a room with lots of windows."

The word "so" shows the relationship between the two parts of this utterance. Interpreters must not only grasp the meaning of the source language but also know how to use target language forms which express the meaning in the most natural way. They need to be aware of characteristics of the English language that affect an interpretation. Larson (1998) identifies one such characteristic of language called packaging, which refers to how meaning is divided up among words. Larson states that an interpreter

> "will often find that there is no exact equivalent between the words of one language and the words of another. There will be words which have some of the meaning components combined in them matching a word which has these components with some additional ones" (p. 61).

Different languages can express the same concepts, but their surface structure or form may be very different. Sometimes it is necessary to interpret one word of the source language into several words in the target language. Or what takes several words in the source language may require only one word in the target language. For example, the English equivalent of CAT BABY is "kitten," BROTHER-SISTER is "siblings," and ALTOGETHER WORTH is "price."

Primary and Secondary Meanings

In English, one word can represent several meanings. The word "run" has 54 meanings listed in the dictionary. Words with more than one meaning have what is called a primary meaning and a secondary meaning (Larson, 1998). The primary is that which comes to mind when a word is said in isolation. In English, the word "dog" would connote a four-footed animal that barks. However, like many words, "dog" also has a secondary meaning when used in context with other words. In the sentence "The play was a dog," the word "dog" means "bad," a secondary meaning.

ASL also contains signs that represent several meanings. For example, the sign CONNECT can represent "link," "unite," "belong," "related to," "join," "bind," or "fasten together." The sign COST means the value of something, such as CAR COST WHAT? However, in the sentence I PAY COST THIS YEAR, the secondary meaning is that of paying taxes to the government. Sternberg, in the *American Sign Language Dictionary* (1987), does not state that signs have primary or secondary meanings per se, but rather states that his book includes "new signs and new applications for old ones" (p. vii). The implication is that people might attach only one meaning to each sign, and he wants to avoid that. Interpreters should be aware that the context of a sentence does influence the meaning of a particular sign.

Knowing that words and signs can have primary and secondary meanings is crucial for an interpreter. This concept helped an interpreter during a police interrogation when the Deaf person signed, YESTERDAY COP PREGNANT. The interpreter envisioned a female police officer quite along in her pregnancy having to make an arrest. Confusion reigned until the interpreter remembered the sign PREGNANT is also a slang sign for "busted by the police." The sentence made more sense once the interpreter used the secondary meaning. Using the primary meaning of the sign would have produced an incorrect literal interpretation. Recognizing the sign's secondary meaning enabled the interpretation to be meaning-based.

Other examples of signs with primary and secondary meanings are:

PROBLEM	problem/issue
FACE-TO-FACE	face-to-face/approach
STUCK	stuck/pregnant

Challenging ASL Structures

Some features of ASL that do not exist in English, such as body shift, use of space, and classifiers, may make some of the content more difficult to grasp and clearly convey in English. For example:

1. ASL: MOM SAY GO CLEAN ROOM (body shift left, look up) NO I WANT PLAY

   English: Mom said go clean the room. No, I want to play.

2. ASL: MY FRIEND HAVE PICTURE (use flat hand to indicate a row of three pictures on the wall with a row of two pictures under it.)

   English: My friend has pictures on the wall

3. ASL: KITCHEN BEAUTIFUL HAVE WOOD TABLE 5 flat-hand CL, CHAIR CL: (show two chairs on either side of the table facing each other)

   English: The kitchen is beautiful with a wood table and chairs

The three English sentences above do not preserve the true meanings. The first sentence with the body shift indicates that the daughter is responding. This information needs to be included in the English interpretation.

English: Mom said to go clean my room, and I said, "No, I want to play."

In the two examples, the number and order of the pictures on the wall or the positioning of the chairs may be important to the message.

Being Aware of Assigned English Words

Often, interpreters will hear an English word and assign it a sign that has a primary meaning other than what would be the equivalent to the English word. For example:

WITHDRAW	withdraw/abstain from voting

During a board meeting, an interpreter used the sign WITHDRAW to show the concept of the word "abstain." Later, in the same meeting, the Deaf consumer signed back to the interpreter the same sign the interpreter had used. The interpreter saw this sign, forgot about its secondary meaning, and interpreted the primary meaning by saying "I withdraw," rather than "I abstain." When this happened, the hearing consumers probably thought the Deaf person had misunderstood the word or the question. Actually, he merely used the same sign the interpreter had used in his response. The interpreter gave a wrong interpretation to the meaning of the sign, causing the Deaf person to look like he was in error.

Summary

It is impossible to do a word-for-sign interpretation that makes sense to an English speaker because ASL and English use different grammar and syntax. Language is not simply made up of words, but also contains metaphors, idioms, and culturally derived phrases. As interpreters render a message from the source to the target language, the form or surface structure of the target language will be different from that of the source language, but the meaning should remain constant.

There are different levels of interpretation:

- **Literal**. This is a word-for-word interpretation. Whatever is said in the source language is brought over verbatim into the target language. This type of interpretation is unnatural and hard to understand.

- **Modified literal**. The grammar is modified to use acceptable sentence structure of the target language, but the lexical items are interpreted more literally.

- **Idiomatic**. This type of interpretation takes the concepts found in the source language and uses natural forms found in the target language. Grammatical presentation and choice of lexical items are meaning-based, not form-based.

- **Unduly free**. This occurs when extraneous information is added to the message which is not found in the source language. The resulting interpretation changes the meaning to either have a stronger or weaker impact than that given.

The more processing of the source material an interpreter does, the greater the likelihood that the message will be conveyed in idiomatic English. There are four levels of processing: lexical, phrasal, sentential, and textual. By knowing the goals, objectives, and intent of the speaker, the interpreter can think beyond the words and phrases and work on presenting a clear relationship between the words, phrases, sentences, and paragraphs that comprise the source message.

Certain words in a language have multiple meanings. The primary meaning is the one that comes to mind when a word is said in isolation. The secondary meaning is employed when a word is used in context with other words. Knowing the primary and secondary meanings attached to a word is critical to an accurate interpretation. If an interpreter uses only the primary meaning of a word when the secondary meaning is intended, the meaning will be lost or skewed. The comment often heard when this occurs is, "The interpreter is glossing, not interpreting." The Deaf consumer frequently chooses to use the same sign that the interpreter used during an interpretation for a specific concept. Error in interpretation occurs when the interpreter glosses the word for its primary meaning in ASL and does not apply the secondary meaning given to the Deaf consumer previously. The goal of any interpretation is to keep the same meaning present in the source language when delivered in the target language and provide as close to an idiomatic interpretation as possible.

Activity 3-1

Paraphrasing

Read the following sentences and paraphrase the underlined portion. An opposite statement can be made; different words can be used; one word can replace several words; or several words can replace one word.

Create different ways the sentence can be restated and still retain the same meaning, taking note of how the underlined portion of the sentence has changed. Share the results with the class.

Example (1):

It helped **that he took beginning math last year.**
It didn't hurt that he took beginning math last year.
Taking beginning math last year helped him.

Example (2):

I was up all night.
I didn't sleep all night.
Last night I couldn't sleep.

Sentences:

A. I can't go until I finish my homework.

B. Grades will be available after June 12.

C. I have three brothers and sisters.

D. I am busy all the time.

E. I want the text done with no decorative print.

F. The long vest was made without sleeves.

G. There were a lot of pretty colors on her dress.

H.   It was <u>hardly raining</u>.

I.   Bill <u>got twenty</u> and Sally <u>got four less</u>.

J.   She was given <u>one-half of the profits</u>.

K.   The time is <u>15 before 5</u>.

L.   He was <u>not a very tall man</u>.

M.   <u>They broke up</u> because he didn't like her cat.

N.   The program <u>was set up 2 decades ago</u>.

O.   The chemical will dissolve, <u>and you won't be able to see it</u>.

Activity 3-2

In-class assignment

Some signs have close equivalents in English, but English may use a different word when in a relationship with another word. The sign CONNECT means two parts that come together as one. The sign CONNECT may mean a "relationship" when between two people, but may mean "join" when showing two groups coming together. For this exercise, pick the appropriate English word that would be used for the sign gloss. Answers are given on the following page.

Sign GROUP

GROUP of cows _____(herd)_____ .

GROUP of geese _____ .

GROUP of Indians _____ .

GROUP of students _____ .

Sign ESTABLISH

Walls are _____.

Houses are _____.

Businesses are _____.

Families are _____.

Rules are _____.

Congressional laws are _____.

Sign EARN

We _____ $3,000 in the fundraiser.

We _____ $550 in the raffle.

We _____ from the sale of our house.

Our business _____ $46,000.00 last year.

Sign MANAGE

The king _____ his kingdom.

The teacher _____ her classroom well.

Answers:

GROUP

    Gaggle of geese

    Tribe of Indians

    Class of students

ESTABLISH

    Walls are erected.

    Houses are built.

    Businesses are formed or set up.

    Families are created.

    Rules are enacted.

    Congressional laws are passed.

EARN

    Fund-raisers raise money.

    Raffles take in or earn.

    You profit from the selling of a house.

    Our business earned a profit.

MANAGE

    Kings rule over their kingdoms.

    Teachers run their classroom.

Activity 3-3

Individual exercise

Change the following sentences to a more idiomatic form. Possible answers are on the next page.

Example:

There are only two things guaranteed in life, demise and government charges. (death and taxes)

1. I need to tell you something that is really bothering me.

2. We rode the train until we couldn't go any further.

3. If you think John will pay you back, the wait will be very long.

4. Don't worry about it now; we will worry about it later when it comes up.

5. Those two are always together, and very similar.

6. The profits on my stock were increasing a lot.

7. Bill is very awkward and clumsy.

8. I know you think it is wrong, but you need to act more maturely.

Answers

1. I need to tell you something that is *really bugging me*.

2. We road the train until the *end of the line*.

3. If you think John will pay you back, *you'll be waiting forever*.

4. Don't worry about it now, we will worry about it *when the time comes*.

5. Those two are always together *like two peas in a pod*.

6. The profits on my stock were *off the charts*.

7. Bill is *a doofus*.

8. I know you think it is wrong, but *you need to grow up*.

Activity 3-4

Individual exercise

Replace the underlined portion of the following sentences with an idiomatic expression listed below. Each sentence may need to be modified.

1. _____ He was very brave, but spiders <u>scared him to death</u>.

2. _____ He felt, while driving his SUV, like <u>he could do anything he wanted</u>.

3. _____ Susan found that class <u>very easy</u>.

4. _____ The twins were <u>very different</u>.

5. _____ Do <u>whatever you want</u>.

6. _____ The idea was not successful, so the group had <u>to start over again</u>.

7. _____ He is a <u>nuisance and bothers me all the time</u>.

8. _____ He tried to find out all the <u>gossip</u> about the Governor.

9. _____ I <u>thought and thought</u> all afternoon.

10. _____ This is not just affecting the people up north, but it will affect <u>everyone</u>.

11. _____ <u>He acts just like his father</u>.

12. _____ The house <u>is from</u> the Civil War era.

13. _____ She was the teacher's <u>favorite</u>.

14. _____ He was sent to the boss' office and <u>yelled at</u>.

15. _____ You need to <u>accept the consequences</u>.

a. King of the road
b. Piece of cake
c. Achilles' heel
d. Carte blanche
e. Like night and day
f. Called on the carpet
g. A chip off the old block
h. Teacher's pet
i. Face the music
j. Dates back to
k. Dirt
l. Racked my brains
m. Go back to the drawing board
n. Every Tom, Dick and Harry
o. Gets on my nerves

16. _____ My son is a problem; the situation is a <u>continual bother to me.</u>

17. _____ You <u>blab all my secrets</u>.

18. _____ I saw you <u>clearly</u> do it.

19. _____ We need to <u>stop fighting and be friends again</u>.

20. _____ With the project, I <u>felt unsupported and helpless</u>.

21. _____ He's great around the house; he <u>can fix everything</u>.

22. _____ <u>Watch</u> for the bus.

23. _____ The boy tried to fool his parents <u>and pretended to cry</u>.

24. _____ Let the <u>people in charge</u> make the decision.

25. _____ I am <u>not feeling very well today</u>.

26. _____ When the guards weren't looking, we <u>ran and escaped</u>.

27. _____ Without fail, this happens to us <u>every year</u>.

28. _____ Would you <u>listen to my story</u>?

29. _____ He passed the test <u>easily and scored high</u>.

30. _____ I <u>tossed and turned</u> all night.

31. _____ You are <u>wrong in your assumption</u>.

32. _____ The speaker <u>talked a lot and very, very fast</u>.

a.	Kiss and make up	j.	Made a run for it
b.	Was left high and dry	k.	With flying colors
c.	Have a big mouth	l.	Didn't sleep a wink
d.	Shed crocodile tears	m.	Year in and year out
e.	In broad daylight	n.	Lend an ear
f.	Powers that be	o.	Thorn in my side
g.	A jack-of-all-trades	p.	Talked a blue streak
h.	Under the weather	q.	Off base
i.	Keep an eye out		

Idioms found in *Phrases and Idioms*, by R. Spears, 1998.

Chapter Four

Fingerspelling in ASL-to-English Interpreting

American Sign Language is made up of a combination of signs, non-manual markers, and finger-spelled words. Seven to ten percent of everyday ASL discourse is composed of fingerspelling (Padden, 1991). It is an established part of the language and is used in ASL to convey certain types of information (Smith, 1988; Battison, 1978; Wells, 1983):

- Proper names—people, places, movie or book titles, brand names

- Names of cities and state abbreviations

- Acronyms of organizations

- Specific terms, such as #CHILD

- English words that have no ASL lexical equivalents

- Technical English terms

Interpreters providing an English interpretation need to have an understanding of how finger-spelling fits into the signed message. Interpreter trainees and interpreters "ask more frequently for repetition of fingerspelled words and manually signed numbers than for other message features such as signs, gestures, etc." (Wells, 1983, p. 147). Because fingerspelling is part of the whole message (Bahleda, 1997), contextual clues may help the interpreter grasp a fingerspelled word.

An interpreter normally works within a context of a specific topic. Keeping this in mind, he or she can then decipher fingerspelled words based on that context. A fingerspelled word can be better understood by focusing on the complete message, using closure and prediction (Bahleda, 1997). Groode (1992) emphasizes the three "C's": context, configuration, and closure. The more familiar with a topic an interpreter is, the more familiar the fingerspelled words are likely to be. Also, if the interpreter is familiar with the vocabulary related to the topic, a partially fingerspelled word will be easier to read.

Prediction, inference, and background knowledge are tools that help the interpreter better read fingerspelling. Every topic has with it a set of words that can be expected to appear. For example, if someone is talking about his trip to the zoo and all the different animals he saw, he might finger-spell a word beginning with the letter Z. The interpreter can infer that this word is "zebra," as there is no other common animal name that begins with the letter Z. If the topic is about different types of computers and hardware, words that may appear are "Macintosh," "personal computer" or "PC," "Intel," or "modem." Prior knowledge of the topic or the use of prep time will help the interpreter think of words that may come up during a presentation. This prep work helps to narrow down the possibilities of which fingerspelled words are likely to appear.

In order to know what word is being fingerspelled, Wells (1983) suggests trying to read the signer's lips if the words are mouthed. One may not be able to read the fingerspelling alone, but by reading the lips, a person might be able to determine the syllables that make up the word.

Lexicalized Fingerspelling

Lexicalized fingerspelled words are "words that are fingerspelled but undergo a systemic, phonological, morphological and semantic change" (Battison, 1978). These fingerspelled words are characterized by:

- **Letter deletion**. A lexicalized word will have one or more letters missing. The word "job" is produced with only the letters J and B. The word "back" is fingerspelled with only the B-C-K.

- **Special movement**. Fingerspelling normally has very little movement, but with lexicalized fingerspelled words, a special movement is incorporated. The word E-A-R-L-Y has a circular movement; B-C-K has a movement either towards the signer or toward the subject or object of the sentence.

- **Altered palm orientation**. In lexicalized fingerspelling, the palm does not face outward all the time. With the word "job," the palm twists around, and the B faces the signer. With the word "what," the palm faces upward as it is fingerspelled.

Lexicalized fingerspelling is utilized by a majority of Deaf ASL users. Knowing what words might be lexicalized and looking for the related movement helps the interpreter recognize these fingerspelled words.

Overall Shape or Individual Letters

Sometimes an ASL user will use letter deletion with words that are not commonly thought of as being lexicalized. Deaf adults who are fluent fingerspellers have been shown to keep the overall shape of the word, but not the shapes of the individual letters (Akamatsu, 1989). It is widely believed that people who are fluent in reading fingerspelling do not read individual letters, but rather see the shape of the whole word (Mendoza, 1999; Akamatsu & Stewart, 1989; Groode, 1992; Haber, 1971).

Patrie (1989) holds a somewhat different view in her research on rapid serial visual processing (RSVP), stating that to be successful in fingerspelled word recognition, a person must have effective processing of rapidly presented visual information. Because each letter is executed separately, each one can be thought of as a separate sign. Taken together, these individual letters form words. The whole word is never seen as one entity, but is composed of individual letters, which require rapid serial visual processing to decipher. However, a person does not need to see each letter to understand a fingerspelled word. When one or more letters is missed, the remaining letters or the rest of the sentence may give a clue as to what the word could be (Guillory, 1966). Consider the sentence

The farmer put the horse in the #b__n"

By using context, it is possible to fill in the blanks and know the horse is in the "barn."

Every fingerspelled word may not continue to be fully fingerspelled throughout a lecture or interpreting event. It may go through a transformation in which letters are deleted. Vowels may disappear, or certain letter combinations may not be fully presented. Reading fingerspelled words with letters deleted is not as difficult as one might think. Imagine interpreting for a college class learning about the planets and the solar system. Even though there are no signs for the different planets, most have a different beginning letter. When the Deaf student wants to find out information during the lecture and signs, "I WANT ASK ABOUT #JPTR, the interpreter, even with deleted or missed letters, can use the context to realize that the student is asking a question about Jupiter.

Akamatsu (1989) states that if the expectation of fingerspelled words is a one-by-one representation of the letters following the printed word, then a person may be looking for something that is usually not there. Throughout a presentation, a fingerspelled word may begin to be presented with letters blended or deleted.

In another example, perhaps a man is talking about a trip he and his wife are taking across the United States. He likes to camp, but his wife likes to stay at hotels. At the beginning of the story, the man fingerspells the complete word #HOTEL but later spells only #HOTL. By the end of the story, he only uses the letters #HTL to represent the concept of the hotel. Interpreters may think they did not catch all the letters in the word, when in fact the Deaf consumer is deleting them. Even with letters deleted, the remaining letters still render the word recognizable. Because fingerspelled words are representative of a concept, they should not be thought of as representing a printed English word.

When a Classifier Replaces a Fingerspelled Word

A fingerspelled word may sometimes be replaced with a classifier. To do this, a signer fingerspells the word and then immediately produces a classifier which will then represent that specific word throughout the remainder of the discourse. For example in the sentence,

MY FRIEND ME GO-TO RIVER FOR K-A-Y-A-K CL:3

the CL:3 replaces the fingerspelled word, K-A-Y-A-K. When interpreting into English, this sentence should not be interpreted as, "my friend and I went to the river to kayak, or boat." The fingerspelled word and CL:3 represent the same concept. The CL:3 is the classifier that will be used later in the story to represent a kayak. When the speaker subsequently signs CL:3, the interpreter should say "kayak" and not "boat."

During a signed discourse, a classifier may be presented immediately before or after a fingerspelled word. The combination of CL/fingerspelled word, or fingerspelled word/CL, gives clarity to the meaning of the classifier.

Because a classifier will often replace a noun, the fingerspelled words that are to be replaced by classifiers are usually nouns. The interpreter can then make an educated guess if a fingerspelled word is missed or unclear. Another example of this during the story of the two people going kayaking is,

LATER WE PASS PEOPLE R-F-T CL: CC.

#RFT does not make a word in English, but an educated guess of "raft" would be a word that would appropriately be replaced by the classifier, CL:CC. Once the noun has been replaced with a classifier, the classifier can also be used to represent a verb. The following sentence,

RIVERCL:3 (go forward then turn left)

would be interpreted as "the kayak followed the bend in the river."

When a Sign Replaces a Fingerspelled Word

Fingerspelled words can also be replaced with signs. This is referred to as "flagging" (Davis, 1989) and involves presenting a fingerspelled English word with a sign that will then represent that word in the spoken interpretation. Often, the sign represents a secondary meaning of the particular word.

Once a sign has been flagged, the replaced English word is retained as the word to use for the rest of the interpretation, unless otherwise noted by the presenter.

One example of flagging is from a Deaf individual who attended an environmental conference and presented on a bird's habitat. Instead of fingerspelling the word #HABITAT continually throughout the presentation, the Deaf presenter flagged the sign HOME to represent the English word "habitat." Every time the flagged sign HOME was used, the interpreter used the English word "habitat," which had been flagged and not the primary meaning of the sign, "home."

In business meetings, Deaf professionals may flag the sign PROBLEM with the fingerspelled word #ISSUE, as they want to use the same professional terminology as others at the meeting. By flagging the sign PROBLEM, the speaker clarifies for the interpreter the exact English word desired to represent a particular sign. After working with a Deaf individual for a while, the interpreter would be familiar with which English words should be attached to particular signs. Until then, when the Deaf consumer is unsure of which English word the interpreter might use, he or she may flag a sign for the specific English word desired.

Name Signs

There is no English equivalent for the ASL concept of a name sign. A name sign is a signed representation of an English name and may fall under two basic types, descriptive and arbitrary (Supalla, 1992). A descriptive name sign (DNS) refers to a physical characteristic used to identify a person. For example, if the person has a large, shaggy moustache, the name sign may be a G moved over half the lip. In a study in which 450 ASL name signs were collected, only 19 percent fell under the DNS category (Meadow, 1977). An arbitrary name sign (ANS) follows a system of using the first letter of a person's name placed in certain locations in sign space.

Supalla's *The Book of Name Signs: Naming in American Sign Language* (1992) cites three types of ANS:

- **ANS in neutral space**. The name sign takes the first letter of the English name and is shaken slightly in front of the signer.

- **ANS with single location on body**. The name sign takes the first letter of the English name and places it on a location of the body. The contact movement is repeated. The areas used can be, but are not limited to, the forehead, the side of the mouth, or over the heart.

- **ANS with dual locations of body**. Using the first letter of the English name, the name sign touches two locations on the body. The movements can be, but are not limited to, movement from the chin to the chest, or from the forehead to the chin.

Some famous people, such as Abraham Lincoln, Adolf Hitler, and George Washington, have established name signs. For people who do not have a name sign, Deaf people will often fingerspell the name and follow it immediately with a name sign they have invented. Supalla's book is an excellent resource for understanding more about name signs.

Because the English language has nothing comparable to name signs, voicing the words "the name sign is" will have no meaning to an English-speaking audience. The only times an interpreter would mention name signs would be if the Deaf consumer was talking about his or her place in Deaf culture or if the audience was composed of ASL students.

Interpreters may want to keep a pad of paper with them, or with the team interpreter, so that when a name sign comes up, they can jot down the name and the name sign. When the name sign comes up again, the interpreter can look quickly at the note pad, or can be cued by the team member. A name sign may also be represented by a title or relationship such as a doctor, a teacher, or a family member. If a Deaf individual is telling about growing up with her brother Fred, whose name sign is F on the forehead, when the name sign comes up, the interpreter may interchange the name "Fred" with the words "my brother."

Fingerspelling Accompanied by a Description

If there is no standard sign equivalent in ASL for an English word or term, a Deaf person might fingerspell the English word, called a "loan word," and then give an explanation, such as

R-S-V-P, YOU CALL TELL-ME COME NOT COME WHICH.

In this situation, the interpreter should choose to simply say, "RSVP," and omit the definition. When an interpreter makes the decision to leave out an explanation, two questions concerning the decision should be asked:

1. Would an average English speaker be aware of the fingerspelled term, and thus not need the explanation?

2. Even if the answer is yes to the first question, is there too much "dead air" time in which the interpreter is not speaking, leaving the audience wondering why the interpreter has stopped talking?

If the interpreter needs additional time to catch up with the signed message, this would be the perfect time to do so if the answer to question one is yes.

Stauffer's (1991) article on visualization cites an example when a Deaf person describing an accident first identified the car by fingerspelling E-L C-A-M-I-N-O. The man further described the car as "half-truck" and "half-car," and then went on further to describe the shape and outline of the car. The description was placed there to express the concept of the El Camino, and did not need to have all the signs describing the vehicle interpreted into English, as this much detail is not common in English discourse. Again, by asking the two questions above, the interpreter can make conscious decisions about what the English-speaking consumer would need in order to make sense of the message.

Interpreters must always take into account whether the information is really necessary. They must decide if what is being signed provides too much detail, which might overwhelm the English speaker's ability to understand the complete message, or if the explanation might insult the intelligence of English-speaking consumers. However, there may be times when too much "dead air" occurs, which may make the English-speaking consumer uncomfortable. The problem with "dead air" time can often be observed in a classroom situation. Take note on how seldom English-speaking teachers stop talking when in front of a class. Even when teachers are looking for an item, they continue speaking to the class. This continuous talk does not occur because the teacher has anything brilliant to say. Rather, if the teacher were to stop talking, he or she may lose control of the class. Interpreters may also need to avoid long periods of silence in their English interpretations.

Acronyms and Abbreviations

At times when interpreting into English, Deaf individuals will use acronyms. Two problems with acronyms are that often the interpreter is seeing letters when expecting a word, or the interpreter is unfamiliar with the acronym. There are ways to improve the ability to interpret acronyms. The interpreter can make a conscious effort to listen for acronyms the English speakers use, look over handouts for acronyms and become aware of acronyms and abbreviations that are common to the field, class, or industry in which the Deaf person is working or involved. Sometimes it helps in a meeting or a classroom situation to have a notepad. When acronyms come up, a team partner, or if working alone, the interpreter can write them down so that the acronyms become more ingrained on the conscious level.

When acronyms are well known to the Deaf community, but not to someone outside of the Deaf community, the interpreter aids the English-speaking individual by expanding the individual letters of the acronym to the word each letter represents. For example if a Deaf individual signs, I MEMBER #NAD, the English interpretation would be "I am a member of the National Association of the Deaf."

In an educational setting, such as the sciences, there are many abbreviations used. Becoming familiar with them will aid the interpreter's ability to voice smoothly when a student is asked to read back a formula, such as:

NA (sodium) + K (potassium) is a dangerous combination.

Summary

Fingerspelling is an established part of ASL and makes up seven to ten percent of the language. Interpreters need to recognize certain aspects of fingerspelled words. They are used to represent:

- Proper names such as people, places, movie and book titles, brand names

- State abbreviations and city names

- Specific terms

- English words that have no ASL lexical equivalents

- Technical English terms

- Acronyms of organizations and businesses

All fingerspelled words are not produced in the same manner. Some words are lexicalized; they undergo systemic, phonological, morphological, and semantic changes which are presented generally in the same way by all ASL users. There are times when a Deaf consumer will spell a word repeatedly throughout a presentation. At the start, the word will be fingerspelled completely, but later letters will be deleted while the overall shape of the word is retained. The shortened version still represents the concept of the original word.

Other times, a fingerspelled word will be replaced with a classifier. When this occurs, the interpreter does not say the word twice, but only provides an English interpretation of the concept represented by the classifier. The same thing occurs when a fingerspelled word is replaced with a sign, or flagged.

Name signs have no equivalents in English. ASL name signs are either descriptive or arbitrary. Because there is neither equivalency nor any meaning connected to a name sign itself, the interpreter does not need to describe it. The interpreter may interpret the appropriate English name or the relationship the person holds with the signer.

There are certain terms or concepts that are common to English speakers that may be described in more detail in ASL. These terms may not need to have the full description interpreted into English. To make that decision the interpreter should ask two questions:

1. Would an average English speaker be aware of the fingerspelled term, and thus not need the explanation?

2. Even if yes, is there too much "dead air" time when the interpreter is not speaking that an audience would wonder why the interpreter has stopped talking?

Being aware of acronyms and abbreviations related to a field, class, or industry helps the interpreter have a smoother delivery of the English interpretation. When interpreting into English, if an acronym used is common within the Deaf community, the English speaker may have no idea what the acronym means. Therefore, to ensure the English-speaking consumer has an equivalent message, the interpreter may need to expand the information and give the full title of the organization or agency.

Activity 4-1

Prediction Exercise

Step 1:   Working with a partner, imagine being assigned to interpret in the following situations. List 5-10 words that may appear in each situation.

Step 2:   Circle the words which may be fingerspelled.

Step 3:   In class, share the answers.

Example: In a college public speaking class, a Deaf student sharing an experience about an overnight camping trip up in the mountains for a leadership class.

Tent   Supplies   Lantern

BBQ   Coleman   Boots

1.   A presentation by a representative from the phone company explaining services available to senior citizens who are losing their hearing.

2.   An appointment with a bank representative to ask about a home mortgage and general banking services.

3.   A presentation by a Deaf administrator from a local school for the Deaf asking a Kiwanis group for a monetary donation.

4.   A Deaf high school student giving a report on the Lewis and Clark expedition.

5. A board meeting for a disabilities group with a presentation on providing interpreting services to city council meetings.

6. A college lecture on Deaf culture regarding the history of ASL.

7. A workshop on the linguistics of ASL for linguists of all languages.

8. A Deaf employee teaching five co-workers how to use the TDD and relay services.

9. A five-month OB/GYN doctor's visit for a sonogram.

10. A signed rendition of the story "Snow White" for third graders.

Activity 4-2

Watch a signed monologue on videotape and observe what strategies the Deaf signer uses for each fingerspelled word. Write the English gloss for each word fingerspelled in the section below which represents how it was handled later in the presentation.

Fingerspelled the word, then deleted letters:

Fingerspelled and replaced with a classifier:

Fingerspelled and flagged with a sign:

Fingerspelled and replaced with an abbreviation:

Fingerspelled with an explanation:

Activity 4-3

Work in groups of three to four and take 10 minutes to list words Deaf people frequently fingerspell or use acronyms for. Come together as a group and share the information.

Deaf or hearing individuals who do not have name signs

Alexander Graham Bell

_____

_____

_____

Schools for the Deaf

Fremont

_____

_____

Organizations

NAD—National Association of the Deaf

_____

_____

Colleges and Universities

CSUN—California State University, Northridge

Others _____

_____

✋ Chapter Five

Grammatical English Sentences

Knowing a language allows a person to put words together in such a way as to form sentences which express thought. The syntactic rules of grammar specify word order. When a string of words conforms to the syntactic rules of a language, a sentence is grammatical; when it does not, it is considered ungrammatical (Fromkin, 1978).

Because ASL and English employ different modalities and are syntactically unique, interpreters must learn many techniques for interpreting from English to ASL; they must drop the English form while incorporating meaning, incorporating cultural mediation, and using correct ASL grammar and syntax. Sometimes, interpreters forget that because adaptations are necessary when interpreting from English into ASL, these adaptations are also necessary when interpreting from ASL into English.

In order to form grammatically correct English sentences, interpreters need to wait for complete thoughts to be delivered in ASL. A complete thought is not always the same as a complete sentence. By waiting for chunks of information from the ASL message, the equivalent phrase or sentence in English will contain proper vocal inflection and sound idiomatic.

Vocal Inflection

ASL contains non-manual grammatical signals that show if a sentence is a question, a command, or a statement. English also has signals to accomplish this. These signals include using specific words, vocal tone, and inflection. The words, "the new dress," can be perceived in several ways when said in English: a question to a friend, a command to a child, or a statement of fact. When interpreting into English, it is critical that the interpretation not be delivered in a monotone, but with the appropriate tone of voice for the message intended.

Questions

ASL has three types of questions, "yes-no" questions, "wh" questions, and rhetorical questions. A "yes-no" question has the non-manual signals of a raised brow, widened eyes, and frequently the body or the head tilting forward (Cokely, Baker, 1980). The interpreter must note these grammatical signals in order to make the English interpretation sound like a "yes-no" question. ASL discourse may or may not contain a specific sign that indicates that the sentence is a question. Some examples follow:

MY MOTHER HAPPY

YOU HAVE BROWN DOG

MOVIE SATURDAY NIGHT

Any of these sentences could be either a statement or a "yes-no" question. Not incorporating the information contained in the non-manual markers that accompany the sentence could skew the message.

A "wh" question usually has a "wh-sign" (WHY, WHEN, WHERE, HOW, and WHO) placed either at the end or the beginning of an ASL sentence (Cokely & Baker, 1980). The problem with "wh" questions is the "wh" word is frequently signed at the end of a sentence. If the interpreter does not allow adequate processing time, the "wh" question word, which should come at the beginning of an English sentence, is placed last in the English interpretation. For example, YOUR NAME WHAT, might be interpreted as, "Your name is what?" This would not be the best way to ask this question. Saying "Your name is what?" may come off as sounding rude or forgetful. A more idiomatic way to say the sentence is, "What's your name?"

The non-manual signals that accompany "wh" questions, a brow squint and generally a tilting of the head, should be an indication that a "wh" question is occurring. The interpreter should wait to see what the "wh-sign" is, and then interpret the sentence into English with the question word at the beginning of the sentence using the appropriate vocal tone to indicate a question. While one sentence or one question may seem rather easy in isolation, when the question is embedded in longer discourse, the interpreter needs to ensure that the listener is aware that a question is being asked.

A rhetorical question does not function as a real question because the speaker is not actually expecting a response from the listener. Rhetorical questions in ASL start with a statement, followed by the signs WHY, WHAT, WHO, HOW, HOW-MANY, WHICH, WHEN, WHERE, or REASON. After a rhetorical question is asked, the signer answers his or her own question. Rhetorical questions are used more frequently in ASL than in English (Cokely & Baker, 1980). In ASL a rhetorical question generally has the facial markers of a brow raise and frequently a tilting of the head.

Rhetorical questions in ASL have two functions (Marron, 1999):

1. To introduce lexical items
   ME BORN WHERE? SAN DIEGO

2. To function as transition markers
   BIRDS MIGRATE, WHY?

When a rhetorical question is used to introduce a lexical item, the interpreter would interpret the message into a statement instead of a rhetorical question. In the example above, the English interpretation could be "I was born in San Diego." In English, rhetorical questions are not generally used to introduce lexical items. The interpreter must keep this difference in mind; otherwise the interpretation will appear more simplistic than it should be. Using rhetorical questions to mark a lexical item is more often used when telling stories to children, e.g., "And what did Goldilocks see? A little house in the forest." This form is rarely used with adults in more formal discourse.

Rhetorical questions used as transition markers in ASL introduce new topics. This is also a function of some rhetorical questions in English. Eileen Forrestal's video presentation dealing with Deaf people using interpreters introduces her survey findings by signing the rhetorical question THEY TELL ME WHAT? followed by a pause. Then she answers her question. For the rest of the clip, she discusses the comments she received.

The question, THEY TELL ME WHAT? could be interpreted as a rhetorical question, "What did Deaf people tell me?" It could also be better interpreted "and here is what I found out" or "and here is what Deaf people told me." The statements are used to introduce the topic, while the interpreter, aware of how transition markers work, guides the listener to know where the topic is going.

Rhetorical questions in English have more functions than in ASL, but are not used as often in formal settings. As in ASL, when a rhetorical question is asked in English, no response is expected. English rhetorical questions can be used (Larson, 1998):

1. To suggest or command.
    Eric, why don't you clean your room?

2. To rebuke, admonish, or exhort.
    Why are you always bothering your sister?

3. To introduce a new topic.
    So how do birds survive the long migration?

4. To emphasize a known fact.
    How can you plan to go out on Saturday when you know it is your grandmother's birthday?

Negation

In ASL, signs such as NOT, CAN'T, and NONE are used to indicate the negation of a comment. Sometimes signers do not use a negation sign, but instead use non-manual markers such as a head-shake along with a frown, sometimes a brow squint, a wrinkling of the nose, and/or a raised upper lip (Cokely & Baker, 1980). Interpreters cannot assume that an English-speaking person, who relies on auditory cues, will pick up on any of the non-manual clues that seem so apparent to someone comfortable in a culture that uses visual markers.

The impact of a hearing person relying solely on auditory cues was quite apparent in this simple situation. One time, a Deaf individual for whom this author was interpreting, answered a particular question by shaking his head back and forth to indicate a negative answer. At that time, I felt since he was not signing I did not have to express the vocal English equivalent of the negative response and actually say the word "no." The hearing consumer could clearly see the head-shake, which meant the same thing in English and ASL. There seemed no purpose in actually saying "no." I waited for the English-speaking consumer to go on, but there was no response. I waited some more; the interviewer waited, and the Deaf individual shook his head again to indicate a negative response. Again, I said nothing. Finally the interviewer asked, "Well, what did he say?"

When a Deaf person uses a negative headshake as an answer, the interpretation does not necessarily have to consist of a simple "no." For example:

Question: Are you planning to go to the movie tonight?
Response: HEADSHAKE-NO
English interpretation: No, I'm not.

In a more formal setting, by listening to the responses of other English speakers, an appropriate response to the following question might be:

Supervisor: Is that report ready?
Deaf employee: REPORT HEADSHAKE-NO
English interpretation: No, the report is not ready.

In the two examples above, note that there are more English words in the interpretation than there are signs. In fact, no signs were used in the first response, only a non-manual marker. The interpreter does need to vocalize the response in English because the hearing person may not note the movement or may be looking elsewhere than at the Deaf consumer.

If the languages were switched, the following might happen:

Hal: TONIGHT YOU-GO MOVIE?
Sue: No, I'm not.
ASL interpretation: HEADSHAKE-NO

The whole message is contained in HEADSHAKE-NO. In ASL sentences, negation facial markers are produced with the clause or statement that is negated. There may or may not be a sign produced that indicates a negation, or the sign produced may happen so quickly the interpreter is not sure it was produced or not. The interpreter must clue into these negative non-manual markers and interpret the English statements as negative in order to convey the appropriate meaning of the sentence.

I GO CAMP LAST-YEAR (HEAD SHAKE AND FROWN)
I GO CAMP LAST-YEAR (HEAD NOD)

Both sentences utilize the same signs. The only difference is the non-manual marker. The message conveyed in English must be equivalent to the meaning conveyed in ASL. If the information contained in the non-manual markers is not included in the English interpretation, the message will be skewed or lost.

In these examples,

I GO TOMORROW (HEAD SHAKE NEGATIVE)
I NOT GO TOMORROW

both sentences contain the same meaning, even though they do not use the same form. An English interpretation must include a word conveying the concept of "not" for both sentences.

Topic/Comment

During a presentation, there is cohesion and flow from old information to new, often using the topic/comment structure. The topic refers to the item being talked about, and the comment is what is being said about it. The topic is what determines how the information that follows will be presented. Interpreters who are unclear of the topic or when it changes may skew the message.

ASL statements often contain the topic first, followed by the comment (Cokely & Baker, 1980). The topic may be part of a sentence, but often it will be a statement that introduces discourse, which will then include comments on the topic. In longer discourse, the topic is stated first and is either followed by a statement, many statements, or a question. This is similar to English, in which the topic sentence is considered the controlling idea, and all sentences that follow either elaborate or qualify it (Hodges, 1982).

On a sentential level, a signer may introduce a topic first, followed by commentary. A problem may occur if an interpreter has not allowed adequate processing time. The object, which is the topic, is stated first, followed by the subject, verb, and a temporal adverb. For example, CAMPING, ME GO YEARLY, interpreted as "Camping, I go every year," is clearly not idiomatic English. A better interpretation would be "I go camping every year."

Topics and Word Choice

Larson (1984) states that topics in English may have specific lexical items that relate to each other. When talking about a king, it must be stated that he *rules* over his *kingdom* while he and his *queen* live in a *castle*. A king would not "manage his area," and he and his "wife" don't live in a "big fancy house." Once the interpreter knows the topic, he or she must keep in mind the appropriate English words that match the particular topic, even though the sign produced may be the same across different situations.

Certain English words belong only with certain topics, yet signs may be carried over from one topic to another. If the signs CONTROL + AGENT were used in a discussion about business, the English equivalent may be "manager," while if the same signs were used in a school, the English term might be "administrator." In a classroom situation, while studying the issue of slavery before the Civil War, this same sign may represent "master." When seeing the sign, the interpreter must be aware of which English word relates with each topic in English. Simply glossing the primary meaning associated with a sign is not appropriate.

Verb Tense

ASL and English handle tense differently (Solow, 1981). The English verb form itself denotes the past, present, or future tense (Humphrey & Alcorn, 1995). Verbs in ASL are not modified like English to indicate tense; the time indicator is not embedded within the verb. Instead, it is stated separately to establish a time frame, and the verbs following remain in that time frame until a new time indicator is stated (Humphrey and Alcorn, 1994). For example, if a person is signing about his childhood and is describing what it meant to grow up as the only Deaf person in a hearing family, he might start the sequence with "GROWING UP" or "LONG TIME AGO." Then when he signs,

    I GO INSTITUTE

he is referring to an event that occurred in his past, and GO would be interpreted as "went." If later in the monologue the signer signs,

    NOW I GO COLLEGE

the interpreter would state, "I am presently attending college." Note the verb forms are identical in both ASL sentences, yet the English interpretation is different. Another example is a Deaf woman signing about when she was eight years old:

    FOR CHRISTMAS I WANT DOLL

The interpreter would say, "for Christmas I *wanted* a doll," as it was in the past, and would not say, "I want a doll." The misinterpretation of tense would confuse the English-speaking consumer.

Distributional Aspect

The distributional aspect in ASL refers to movements that occur with verbs to indicate how an action is performed or distributed (Cokely & Baker, 1980). By changing the direction of movement for a verb, the signer can show if an item is distributed to one person or to several people. This distributional aspect does not occur in English. In the following two sentences,

"I gave my sister a book" or
"I gave each of my students a book"

the English verb "gave" does not change, but a modifier, such as "each" must be included to convey the meaning from ASL.

Another example is a Deaf individual who was looking for a particular item and had called around to different stores, only to be told none of them carried it. To show a negative response from every store, the person signs

CALL-Lft, NO-TO-ME, CALL-middle, NO-TO-ME, CALL-Rt., NO-TO-ME.

A literal English interpretation would be, "I called one place; they said 'no.' I called another place; they said 'no.' I called another place; they said 'no.'" To produce a more idiomatic interpretation, the distributional aspect of the ASL verb CALL, produced three times, could be compressed into the English verb "called" and said only once, with the interpretation being presented as: "Everywhere I called, I got the same answer, no."

This idiomatic interpretation retains the meaning, but the information of calling more than one store in ASL is expressed in the English word "everywhere." The interpreter keeps in mind how English presents concepts, using very different linguistic structures than ASL.

Summary

ASL uses non-manual markers to convey certain information and differentiate between statements, questions, and commands.

It has two types of questions with different non-manual facial markers. "Yes-no" questions have the non-manual signals of a raised brow, widened eyes, and often a forward head tilt. "Wh" questions use specific signs, which can be placed at the beginning or end of a sentence. The signs are accompanied by the non-manual signal of a brow squint. If the non-manual signals that accompany questions are noted, with or without a question sign, the interpreter should be aware that a question is occurring.

Rhetorical questions are not really questions but serve a different function than asking for information. These questions can introduce lexical items or serve as transition markers. Rhetorical questions in ASL can be interpreted into English as statements, as topic sentences to introduce the next segment of the presentation or, rarely, as rhetorical questions.

In ASL, negative sentences may be formed by using a negation sign, such as NOT, CAN'T, or NONE, and/or by the signer using a headshake, a frown, sometimes a brow squint, a wrinkling of the nose, and/or a raised upper lip. Some questions can be simply answered by a headshake, but the English interpretation should include a spoken word or words.

In ASL, a topic is the main idea that will be discussed. Once a topic has been introduced, a statement, many statements, or a question will follow in support of the topic. Not only must the interpreter be clear when a new topic is introduced, he or she must also keep in mind the appropriate English vocabulary that is associated with that particular topic. An identical sign may be produced from one topic to the next, but the English word choice might be different, depending on the topic.

ASL and English handle verb tense differently. In English, the verb itself denotes tense. Verbs in ASL do not change to indicate tense because the time indicator is a separate lexical item. Once a time frame has been established in ASL, all verbs from that point forward will remain in the same tense and must be interpreted as such into English.

Activity 5-1

Interpret the following rhetorical questions into appropriate English. One student will sign each sentence while another renders an English interpretation as a statement. A third student could be used to listen to the interpretation and give feedback.

1. NEXT PRESIDENT WHO? CONNIE

2. ME ARRIVE HOUSTON TIME 7 HOW? TRAIN

3. MARY CAN'T PLAY TOMORROW WHY? #LEG BROKE

4. BOY, (index, 1ft) HISTORY CLASS GOT D WHY? NOT DO RESEARCH PAPER

5. I GO-TO WORK LATE, TIME? 10 NIGHT

6. I LATE REASON? MY OTHER APPOINTMENT POSTPONE

7. SPECIAL VISITOR NEXT WEEK WHO? MY BROTHER FROM NEW YORK

8. HATE GO-TO WORK SATURDAY WHY? MUST ARRIVE TIME 5 MORNING

9.   I PLAN MY SUMMER VACATION WHERE? DISNEYLAND

10.   MY FATHER HURT #ARM HOW? PLAY BASKETBALL

Activity 5-2

This activity looks at the ability to interpret "wh" questions appropriately as part of a larger discourse. One person will sign each statement while a partner interprets the statement into English.

Use a tape recorder and play back the English interpretation. Note the areas in which the English does or does not sound appropriate.

1. I GO COLLEGE. NOW TAKE 15 #UNIT. I GRADUATE NEXT-YEAR. YOU COLLEGE, WHERE?

2. I GO ASL WEEKEND. PLAN MEET MANY PEOPLE. I WILL ARRIVE FRIDAY NIGHT. YOU PLAN GO WHEN?

3. I HAVE WONDERFUL TEACHER. YOUR TEACHER WHO?

4. MY TEACHERS HEARING DEAF BOTH. MY DEAF CULTURE TEACHER, HIMSELF DEAF. FOR INTERPRETING CLASS HEARING. YOUR TEACHER FOR FINGERSPELLING DEAF HEARING, WHICH?

5. LONG-AGO HAPPEN #CIVIL WAR, REASON WHAT?

Activity 5-3

Using only the signs supplied in the exercise, one person should sign each sentence two ways as indicated. A partner will interpret each as either a statement or a question using appropriate vocal tone to indicate sentence type.

Example:

ME HUNGRY	As a declarative statement	I am hungry.
	As a yes/no question	Are you hungry?

1. COME HOME

   As a declarative statement
   As a yes/no question

2. BIRDS FLY SOUTH WHEN

   As a "wh" question
   As a rhetorical question

3. I ENJOY MOVIE

   As a negative sentence
   As an affirmative sentence

4. HAVE MONEY ME

   As a negative sentence
   As an affirmative sentence

5. PEOPLE HERE HAPPY

   As a yes-no question
   As a statement

6. WE HAVE-TO GO HOME, WHY

   As a rhetorical question
   As a "wh"-question

Alternative exercise: Each student would write a sentence that can be presented in two different ways, using the same signs. Present the sentences in front of the class.

Chapter Six

ASL Expansion

Interpreters need to not only be able to comprehend the message being presented in the source language; they also need to be able to identify the speaker's purpose and know how to convey that purpose to the audience. This means being aware of the speaker's perspective and the response the speaker desires from the audience (Seleskovitch, 1978).

To convey the speaker's intentions, interpreters work within the confines of a language's grammar, lexicon, and rules that govern how that language is used. Being aware of the similarities and differences between the features of ASL and English and how each language expresses itself in storytelling, interaction, or formal presentations helps interpreters make the necessary adjustments to the English message in order to convey the meaning more effectively.

Interpreters must take care to avoid interpreting ASL structures literally into English. English has its own features that emphasize, clarify, or specify information. These features include vocal inflection, modifiers, certain phrases, tone, and word order (Barnwell, 1980).

The interpreter must keep in mind style and syntax differences between English and ASL. Style differences include the use of time referents, tense, the use of space, and direct address (Lawrence, 1994). Lawrence's research identified seven features found in ASL but not in English. These are referred to as ASL expansion and include the following: contrasting, faceting, reiteration, utilizing 3-D space, explaining by example, couching, and describe-then-do.

In 1999, the Regional Interpreter Training Consortium (RITC) produced a small booklet and videotape-based on Lawrence's work which examine how expansion features are best interpreted from ASL to English. If the interpreter does not interpret the discourse style appropriately, the interpreted English message may not be clearly understood by the consumer.

Contrasting

Contrasting in ASL occurs when someone "compares two things by juxtaposing two opposite ideas in order to emphasize one of them" (Lawrence, 1994, p. 207). This is done when a concept is presented in ASL, followed by a negated form of the same concept. Examples of this are:

Concept: a person walking at a normal pace
ASL: point WALK NORMAL, SLOW <u>NOT</u>.

Concept: a clear sliding glass door
ASL: GLASS DOOR CLEAR, CL:F, NONE

Concept: a cold room
ASL: THAT ROOM COLD, WARM NOT

Contrasting is not commonly used in English. English speakers either produce a positive statement or a negative statement about what is being discussed. What might be more idiomatic to an English speaker would be to make one statement of what something is.

ASL: WALK NORMAL, NOT SLOW.
Literal interpretation: The person walked normal, not slow.
Idiomatic interpretation: The person walked as they normally would.

ASL: GLASS DOOR CLEAR, CL:F (both hands), NONE
Literal interpretation: The glass door was clean, no spots.
Idiomatic interpretation: The glass door was spotlessly clean.

ASL: MY ROOM COLD, WARM NOT
Literal interpretation: My room is cold, not warm.
Idiomatic interpretation: My room is really cold.

A sentence dealing with a student who has a stay-at-home mom might be signed:

STUDENT HIS MOTHER STAY HOME, WORK NOT

In English, because information is sometimes implied, the interpretation could be "The student has a stay-at-home mom." This sentence does not include the information that his mother does not work, as that information is implied in the phrase "stay-at-home."

Faceting

Larson (1998) talks about how one concept is a bundle of components that make up meaning. In ASL, faceting is "a feature whereby several different signs are signed sequentially to more clearly express one idea" (Lawrence, 1994, p. 209). Signs used in faceting are different but still somewhat synonymous. These signs are used to narrow down a concept to a more specific image or to convey a single idea. The interpreter may want to present a faceted concept into English by the use of adjectives or adverbs. If the following concepts were described in ASL,

A beautiful sunset
A room in disarray

the signer would use descriptors to establish a picture for the audience. Detailed information in ASL may be conveyed with fewer lexical items in English. For example, a description of a sunset might be signed as follows:

SUNSET BEAUTIFUL RED PURPLE SPREAD WOW

The interpreter could say, "It was a spectacular sunset," and the English speaker would have a clear mental picture of it. Also, the use of tone could enhance the sentence if emphasis were put on the word "spectacular." On the other hand, if the interpreter were to produce a more literal interpretation and said, "the sunset was beautiful, with red and purple spreading out, wow," the interpretation would sound clumsy and unnatural and would not present the image in the listener's mind that the signer intended.

There are times when more English words than signs are required in order to convey an idea, but there are also times when the opposite is true. When a signer uses a number of signs to provide a detailed description of an event or situation, interpreters may be able to pick the one or two words that would bring to mind a clear picture for the English-speaking listener. For example, a room in disarray may be described as follows:

ROOM CLOTHES MESS UP, DESK DRAWERS PULL-OUT, PULL-OUT REMAIN PAPERS CL:B+++ SPREAD DISGUSTED

If the interpreter says, "The room had clothes everywhere; it was messed up; desk drawers were left open, papers spread all over, it was disgusting," the message is not as clear as a more idiomatic interpretation. "The room looked like a tornado hit it" has all the necessary information included.

If an English interpretation takes less time than the ASL message, there is more time to produce a clear interpretation. Trying to catch every sign and assign a word to each one results in an interpretation that is unnaturally fast and contains no pauses. When this occurs, the hearing consumer does not have time to truly digest the information, and would have to work harder to try to decipher its meaning. Interpreters need to think how a concept can be presented in concise, idiomatic English. The English words, though not as many, are equivalent in meaning to all the signs utilized and still give the listener time to pause and comprehend the full message.

Reiteration

"Reiteration refers to signs that are repeated in a text the same way they were initially stated" (Lawrence, 1994, p. 209). A signer may repeat a certain detail in a sentence, or one sign may be used both before and after a concept, much like bookends. This is done in order to emphasize, clarify, heighten, and specify concepts. For example, if a presenter wanted to let the listeners know the story he is about to tell is a really funny story, he might sign:

WANT TELL-YOU FUNNY STORY, FUNNY.

Since the English language does not use this construction, the interpreter may need to eliminate one of the repeated adjectives or combine the adjectives, using just one English term to indicate the concept presented. The word "hilarious" or the phrase "really funny" can represent the bookend signs of FUNNY. Another example might be:

RAIN-ON-ME CLOTHES WET, CHANGE MUST WET

If an ASL sentence incorporates reiteration, the interpreter must find the central concept of the message and use only the words which clearly convey the concept, not a word for every sign.

Utilizing 3-D Space

ASL, being a three-dimensional visual language, uses spatial information that must be taken into consideration when interpreting into English. Not all spatial information needs to be interpreted; the interpreter needs to keep in mind what information is crucial to the message and what information is simply an aspect of ASL that is not necessary in the English interpretation.

An example is a Deaf person describing how she is going to the library (and indexing to the right) and then going to the store (and indexing to the left) and then finally coming home (and signing HERE to indicate home). The information in the ASL message of where the library and store are located does not need to be stated overtly in English. In English we might say something like, "I need to go to the library and then the store before coming home." The additional spatial information, though appropriate in ASL, is not fitting for the English message. Including the English word "before" makes the sentence sound more idiomatic.

Information contained in directional verbs may also not need to be conveyed. For example:

LAST-WEEK, L.A (left). NEW YORK (right), ME FLY (left to right).

When expressing the concept of flying from the West Coast to the East Coast the plane usually flies from left to right. To an English speaker there is little concern how the sign PLANE moves, left to right, right to left, or front to back, because English speakers have no indication of direction in the verb "to fly."

There are times, however, when spatial information is crucial to the message. For example, the exact locations of vehicles or people involved in an automobile accident must be articulated clearly. ASL handles this information efficiently, whereas English usually requires many more words that may or may not convey the information accurately.

As 3-D space is used in ASL to describe a scene or layout and to assign locations to people, things, or ideas, signers "paint a picture" with visual details. Watching such a display is enjoyable for a person who understands the language. English, on the other hand, does not use these features, and interpreting each and every detail may make the interpretation sound very simplistic or overly complex. Interpreters must decide how much of the visual detail is necessary. Too much detail can sound wordy or unnatural and is distracting because English speakers typically rely on far fewer visual details. Too little detail, however, may leave the listener with "dead air." When interpreting information that uses space, it is best to make sure the information is delivered into idiomatic English that is comfortable to an English speaker.

When interpreting spatial information literally, the meaning will be skewed. Humphrey and Alcorn (1995) point out that interpreters working between English and ASL sometimes try to match lexical items instead of striving for message equivalency. An example is when a signer is describing a family packing for a camping trip:

```
CAR-RT PUT-IN (left to right) (non-dominant hand to show listing of items)
TENT, FOOD, SLEEPING #BAGFINISH CAR-DRIVE-OFF
```

The use of space shows the car in one location with the items being placed into it before it drives off. All of this is clear in a visual language. A literal interpretation might be, "The car, which was on the right, we put in the tent, the food, sleeping bag, when we finished, the car drove off to the left."

By looking for the message and utilizing an understanding of the spatial referents used in ASL, an idiomatic English interpretation may be, "After packing the car with our camping gear—tent, food, sleeping bags—we drove off."

The spatial information is not important to the meaning of the story. The items of the tent, food, and sleeping bags were bundled into the words "camping gear," and if there was not enough time to include these details, the interpreter could then choose to omit any or all of the words, "tent, food, and sleeping bags." Other items to note:

- The verb "packing" is used in place of the movement of items into the car.

- The word "after" is used to convey the meaning behind the time indicator FINISH.

- Instead of the car driving off, the statement is "*we* drove off." The idea of the car is implied in the verb "drove."

Couching

"Couching is when background or contextual information is added to a concept to make it clear" (Lawrence, 1994, p. 212). When an item is presented in ASL, background information or a brief description is added in order to make the message more understandable to the recipient. Lawrence (1994) states that since English is a "low-context" language, speakers of English understand one another with a limited amount of information. ASL is a "high-context" language, where much of the information has to be explicit. An interpretation into English must omit the extraneous "high context."

For example, if a signer mentions "call waiting," he may explain the concept to Deaf members of the audience. Hearing audience members, because they are most likely familiar with the concept, would not need the explanation.

Sometimes, a Deaf person fingerspells an English loan word followed by a description of what it means. Here, the interpreter must decide if the English-speaking audience is sufficiently aware of what the loan word means. If so, the interpretation may only include the fingerspelled word with the description omitted. If the description goes on over a period of time, though, and the interpreter had made a conscious decision to omit it, the interpreter must then decide when there is too much dead air time and include a bit of the description. There is a fine line between what to exclude in order to make the language sound idiomatic, and what to include in order to ensure that the audience, who is dependent on auditory stimuli, stays involved.

Explaining by Example

Unlike couching, explaining by example does not give a brief description, but instead, gives a list of examples as an explanation. Some nouns in ASL use representatives to convey a category. For example, the concept of "pets" is conveyed as DOG CAT FISH ETC., and "jewelry" as EARRINGS NECKLACE BRACELET ETC.

The interpreter keeps in mind that ASL tends to use more examples than spoken English. For this reason, every item listed in the examples does not necessarily have to be spoken in the English interpretation, or the examples may not have to be interpreted at all. When the interpreter feels the idea presented in ASL with examples is not one that an English speaker would need an explanation of, interpreting the examples is not necessary. For example, if a Deaf person is talking about fast food and signs, YOU-KNOW MCDONALDS, TACO BELL, WENDYS, the interpreter may be able to just say "fast food places." Another option would be to interpret a couple of the examples presented and then put the remaining items under a general topic.

Describe, Then Do

This feature of ASL occurs when the signer moves from a narrative style of discourse to taking on the role of a person speaking. This is also referred to as direct address, direct dialogue, role shift, or direct discourse. When relating the discourse, the speech is quoted more or less verbatim. Indirect address, or reported speech, involves a person relating what someone has said previously to another person, but presenting the information in a narrative form. For example, if a day earlier a person had overheard John say:

"Mary, will you join me for dinner tonight?"

and later, this person wanted to relay the information to someone else using direct address, the sentence would be,

"Yesterday I heard John ask, 'Mary, will you join me for dinner tonight?'"

This is a direct quote of what John said to Mary.

If the same person wanted to pass on the information using indirect address or a narrative form of discourse, the person would say,

"Yesterday John asked Mary if she planned to join him for dinner that evening."

Because the telling about the conversation occurred on a different day than the one John asked the question, the word "tonight" must be changed to "that evening." Likewise, "tomorrow" would need to be interpreted "the next day," and "yesterday" as "the day before." This is an area in which many students and working interpreters have difficulty.

ASL almost invariably uses direct address to convey what transpired between two or more people. Marron (1999) states that direct address, or direct discourse, occurs less frequently in English than ASL. In English, direct address is used in:

- Story telling, including jokes.

- Discourse to dramatize a point.

- Speaking to children.

Direct address is rarely used in English in formal situations. An exception might be a presenter telling a story or joke at the beginning of a formal presentation to loosen up an audience. When an English speaker does tell a story or a joke, each person in the story is usually identified, and there is often a shift of tone to differentiate the characters.

English speakers tend to use indirect or reported speech more frequently than direct speech. The use of indirect speech in English involves spoken discourse being described without being quoted. For example, "The president said he will visit Africa next month," would be said as opposed to "The president said 'I will visit Africa next month.'" The former statement uses indirect address, the latter, direct speech. When the exact words are important, direct speech would be chosen. Otherwise, the information is expressed in indirect address.

Direct address is used often in ASL in both informal and formal registers. The speaker acts out the role of each character using body shift and gives the information being conveyed in the first person (Marron, 1999). ASL signers employ direct address in three different situations:

1.   To tell a story that involved the signer and one or more other persons.

2.   To tell a story about two or more other people in which the signer was not involved.

3.   To dramatize a monologue.

Therefore, when interpreting from ASL to English, direct address must often be conveyed as indirect address.

Third Person in Personal Stories

Interpreting direct address into indirect address involves changing the second person into third person. This is not an easy task. For example, "Mom told her son, 'I want *you* to drink *your* milk'" would be changed to, "Mom told her son *she* wanted *him* to drink *his* milk." Peterson (2002) noted when he worked with interpreting students and asked them to interpret from ASL to English, the area of direct address caused them difficulty. He found that "the pronominal references are often too subtle for students to catch. They are left with a vague understanding of what was said but not of who said it or to whom" (p. 147).

Another example is,

    BILL INFORM-ME (body shift) I GO VISIT BROTHER SATURDAY

Interpreting the statement into indirect address in English requires the person being spoken about (Bill) to be expressed in the third person. "Bill told me *he* will go visit *his* brother on Saturday." Second person is never used with indirect address.

Introducing Each New Speaker

An interpretation using direct address involves introducing the speaker at the start of each turn. Each time the signer uses a body shift to indicate a different person is saying something, the interpreter could say something such as:

Someone told me
Another person shared
Then Jack said
Another example is
Another response was

The statements listed above are not signed since their meaning is conveyed in the signer's body shift, but they do need to be included in the English interpretation to make clear who is saying what.

Consider the following example:

Eye gaze up little girl talking to mother
MOTHER, FLOWER BRING-YOU

Role shift to become mother, turn body, eye gaze down
SWEET, ME LOVE FLOWERS, WHERE GET?

Role shift to child, turn body, eye gaze up
OUTSIDE

A very literal interpretation, like a dramatic reading, is almost never appropriate:

"Mother, I brought you a flower. Sweet, I love flowers. Where did you get it? Outside."

Remaining in direct address requires the introduction of each speaker:

"The child called out, 'Mother I brought you a flower,' and mother said, 'How sweet. I love flowers. Where did you get it?' The child told her, 'I got it outside.'"

The interpreter may, and probably should, choose to produce the English interpretation employing indirect address, which would be as follows:

"The child told her mother she brought her a flower. The mother thought it was sweet. The mother loves flowers, and asked the girl where she got it. The child told her outside."

Choosing a Direct or Indirect Interpretation

Tipton (2003) notes that if the gender of one of the characters is unknown, direct address should be used. For example,

TEACHER INFORM-ME body shift YOU CHEAT, ME SEE

Since the gender of the teacher is unknown, an interpretation employing indirect address would not work. "The teacher told me he or she had seen me cheating" is awkward compared to "The teacher said, 'I saw you cheating.'" Likewise if the discourse contains profanity or name-calling, indirect address would not capture the entirety of the meaning (Tipton, 2003). For example,

HAL COME-UP-TO-ME body shift DAMN! MY VCR, YOU BROKE, STUPID YOU!

An indirect interpretation would lose some of the impact and content of the message. "Hal came up to me, angrily accusing me of breaking his VCR" is not as strong as "Hal came up to me and said,

'Dammit, you broke my VCR, you idiot!" In deciding whether to use direct or indirect address in an English interpretation, an interpreter must consider:

What type of discourse or register the speaker is using.
Who the audience is.
What the speaker's purpose is.

For example, courtroom interpreting might require a more verbatim rendition while a lecture would lend itself to an indirect style.

In a formal setting, English speakers are accustomed to hearing information in the narrative form using indirect address. When a speaker is referencing another person and the interpreter uses first person, the audience hearing the pronoun "I" may become confused about who said what. The audience may be unclear as to who is actually making the "I" comments, the speaker or the person to whom the speaker is referring. For example, a Deaf speaker is informing a group of individuals about problems Deaf people have encountered when using a particular agency. The Deaf speaker begins to share information learned from a survey questioning 22 Deaf people who had used the agency during the previous year. During the presentation the speaker signs:

```
DEAF TELL ME role shift I FEEL FRUSTRATED, NO INTERPRETER, role shift other
side I WANT WRITE, BUT PEOPLE PATIENT NONE role shift I MEET PERSON THERE SIGN,
YES, BUT FINGERSPELL, FINGERSPELL, FINGERSPELL, I DON'T UNDERSTAND
```

An interpreter using direct address in the English interpretation without introducing each speaker may cause the audience to be unaware of where the comments of the speaker end and the comments of each of the surveyed clients begin. When presented with comment after comment being interpreted in the first person, the English-speaking consumer can soon become lost as to how many people are actually responding.

A successful interpretation is one in which the listeners are able to differentiate between the speaker's personal comments and the comments of other people being referenced. During an exercise with several interpreters who were unable to see the signer quoted above but who were familiar with the interpreting process, not one person listening to the interpreter could tell how many people were involved. One person commented after the exercise that if she had not been told during the introduction of the exercise that the speaker would be listing comments from other people, she would have thought that all the comments were from the speaker because of the use of the pronoun "I." Another person stated he was confused because he didn't know who the "I" represented. These are comments from people who supposedly understand how direct address works in ASL, so one can imagine the confusion experienced by someone unfamiliar with the language.

Instead of using direct address, a more clear interpretation using indirect address, might be: "Several Deaf people shared their experiences with me. One was frustrated because no interpreter was available. One wanted to communicate by writing, but the agency person had no patience for that. Another Deaf person met someone there who could supposedly sign, but because that person fingerspelled practically everything, the Deaf person didn't understand what was being said."

This example reinforces the idea that using indirect address, or reported speech, is the preferred method of conveying the information clearly in English.

Summary

Because English is syntactically different from ASL, interpreters must be aware of style differences in ASL and English discourse. Some features found in ASL but not in English, referred to as "expansion techniques," include the following:

- **Contrasting**. In ASL, a concept is presented, followed by the opposite form of the same concept. English speakers usually either produce a positive or a negative statement about something. The interpreter, seeing two statements that are opposites, would most likely produce one English statement, either positive or negative, that is also idiomatic.

- **Faceting**. This occurs when several different, but related, signs are used in sequence to narrow a concept to a more specific image or to convey a single idea. The concepts being conveyed will usually be interpreted into English as adjectives or adverbs.

- **Reiteration**. This occurs when the signer repeats a certain detail or refers to the main topic in a sentence. English speakers do not do this but use synonyms instead. The interpreter should retain the meaning of the ASL message, but keep in mind how English would present the information in an appropriate linguistic style.

- **Utilizing 3-D space**. In ASL, the space around the signer is used in order to describe a scene or layout and to ascribe location to people, places, or things. Interpreters must decide how much of the visual information is necessary for an auditory listener.

- **Couching**. This refers to a signer providing background information or a brief description of a concept in order to make the signed message clearer to the recipient. A signer may present a fingerspelled word and then give a description of what the word means. The interpreter must decide if the English-speaking audience is sufficiently aware of what the word means and would then only refer to the fingerspelled word, choosing to omit the description. By doing this the interpreter conveys the appropriate message in English.

- **Explaining by example.** This refers to a signer giving a list of examples as an explanation. In English, if a speaker introduces an idea that may require more explanation, he or she may begin the section by saying "in other words," "what I mean," "for example," or "such as." The interpreter could also take the list of items presented and interpret only a couple of the signs and then put the remaining items under a general topic.

- **Describe, then do**. Both English and ASL use direct and indirect speech. Direct speech occurs when a person is quoted more or less exactly. Indirect speech occurs when the information is conveyed as a narrative. Direct address in English is used in storytelling, jokes, to dramatize a point, or when talking with children. Direct address is rarely seen in the formal register in English.

ASL uses direct address quite often. This is also referred to as role taking. Interpreters can take direct address in ASL and interpret it as indirect address in English. This is frequently the clearest, most idiomatic way to interpret this kind of information. An interpreter has three options when handling direct address from ASL into English:

Keep the interpretation literal, like a dramatic reading (almost never appropriate).
Stay in direct address but introduce each speaker.
Move into indirect address.

When interpreting direct address from ASL into reported speech in English, interpreters must be careful to use appropriate pronouns and verb tense.

Activity 6-1

English vocabulary selection
Group and partner work

Find a videotape of signed monologues.

Step 1:   As a group go through the tape and:

Identify types of expansion present.

Decide what the goal of each monologue is.

Discuss what adjustments would be needed in the English interpretation.

Step 2:   Divide into pairs.

Decide which person will do the English interpretation and which person will be listening. Watch the videotaped monologue from step A.

The person listening to the interpretation will not watch the Deaf person signing. He or she should have a paper and pen in order to take notes.

The person doing the English interpretation will watch the videotape, and, using the information discussed in step A, will try to do an idiomatic and appropriate English interpretation.

Afterwards, the partner will share which sections of the interpretation sounded natural, and which did not.

Step 3:   As a group:

Discuss areas that were problematic and those that were handled effectively during the ASL-to-English interpretation.

Discuss ways to overcome the problems.

Incorporate suggestions.

Step 4:   Divide back into pairs, change roles, and repeat steps 2 and 3.

Activity 6-2

Direct and indirect address

The following dialogues have quotation marks around each speaker's words. Some quotes consist of one sentence; others contain two or three sentences.

Step 1:   Divide into groups of three.

Step 2:   One person will sign the sentences in each scenario using appropriate body shift. The person signing should identify the scenario and the people involved. This is done before the interpretation begins.

One person will interpret the signed message into English twice, once using direct speech and once using indirect speech. The third person will listen, but not watch the signs.

Step 3:   After the interpretation, the person who listened will relate how difficult or easy it was to identify when each person was talking. The group should discuss what brought clarity to the message and when the message seemed uncertain.

Step 4:   Change roles, and repeat the exercise.

Step 5:   When all exercises have been interpreted, each student will create an original scenario to sign, following the steps above.

Example of an English interpretation:

Direct: Bob asked Sue, "You want to go to lunch?" She said, "Sure I do."

Indirect: Bob asked Sue if she wanted to go to lunch with him, and she said she did.

1. **Scenario**: A mom talking with her daughter on the phone.
   "You need to be home tonight at 9."
   "But the movie doesn't get over until 9:30. Sally is driving."
   "Can Sally drop you off first? Why don't you call her?
   "Sure. I will call you back in 5 minutes."
   "Who else is going?"
   "Billy. I don't like him, but he's Sally's boyfriend."

2. **Scenario**: A boyfriend talking to his girlfriend.
   "You want to see a movie?"
   "Sure."
   "What movie do you want to see? I want to see the new one."
   "With Jodie Foster? Yeah."
   "What time do you want to go? I'd like to go to the 8 p.m."
   "I have an early class. Let's go to the 6:30 show."

3. **Scenario**: A college student talking with her roommate.
   "I didn't get home until 4 a.m. last Saturday."
   "My mom would kill me."
   "My mom won't find out if you don't tell her. I always get home early when I stay with mom."
   "Don't you love living in the dorm? I've lived here for two years."
   "Next year I plan to look for an apartment. I want more privacy."
   "Not me, I like the dorm."

4. **Scenario**: An employee talking with another employee.
   "I have to go to a meeting tomorrow."
   "What's it about, the new retirement plan?"
   "Yeah, and also about our medical plan."
   "I went to that meeting last week; I learned a lot. Get me another booklet. I lost mine."
   "OK."

5. **Scenario**: Four-year-old Billy talking with his cousin Sally, who is three.
   "Do you want to swing?"
   "You can push me."
   "I don't want to."
   "Then I won't play with you."
   "I want my mommy."

6. **Scenario**: An English teacher speaking to her 7th-grade student.
   "Mario, have you finished your story?"
   "I finished it yesterday. When is the book report due? I think it is due next Monday, but I didn't start that yet"
   "Starting tonight?"
   "I have football practice, maybe tomorrow."
   "This is worth one-third of your grade. I want to make sure you get it in on time."

Chapter Seven

Illocutionary Forces, Register, and Formulaic Elements

Language is made up not only of words, but also how they are put together. The surface structure of a language includes the words and grammar. The deep structure is the semantic structure, or the meaning behind the words. Two areas in which deep and surface structure must be considered have to do with illocutionary forces and register.

Illocutionary Forces

Illocutionary force is the desired effect of a communication; it is the purpose underlying the words, the speaker's intention. When asked to tell what a speaker is saying in a particular sentence, the person listening must be aware of not only the words themselves, but also the intent behind the words (McCawley, 1981).

English sentences are often presented with an illocutionary force behind them (Larson, 1998). Types of illocutionary force include the following:

Statement, intended to give information

Question, intended to request information

Command, to encourage or solicit an action

Threat, to intimidate the listener

Warning, to elicit self-protective behavior in the listener

Promise, to predict action from the speaker

The presence of illocutionary force in a sentence means there is more implied than what appears on the surface. For example, the statement, "Mary and John are getting married," can also be said as follows:

I want to inform you that Mary and John are getting married.

The "I want to inform you" includes what is called a performance verb, implied in the first sentence and overtly stated in the second. ASL is more explicit than English in the use of performance verbs. When interpreting into English, it is possible to leave out the performance verb found in the ASL sentence because the information will be implied in English. In the following example, the performance verb is underlined.

INFORM-YOU, MARY, JOHN, MARRY, WILL

The verb of informing does not need to be interpreted for the listener to have a clear understanding of the meaning and purpose behind the sentence. Omitting the performance verb can also help an interpreter keep up with the signer, since each sign does not need a spoken equivalent to maintain meaning between the two languages.

Sometimes, the purpose behind a sentence and the way the sentence is presented appear contradictory. One example is the use of rhetorical questions. Even though they appear to be real questions, the illocutionary force behind them is different. When a rhetorical question is used to introduce a lexical item, the interpreter would simply interpret the message into a statement.

There may also be times when there is more than one illocutionary force in a statement. For example, the sentence,

"Clean this room or you can't go out and play"

contains two illocutionary forces, "I am commanding you" and "I am threatening you."

If the interpreter decided to delete the performance verb signed in ASL into English, the following sentence,

WARN++ YOU START FIGHT HERE SCHOOL, SUSPEND, WILL

can be interpreted as,

"Get into a fight at school, and you will be suspended."

The idea of a "warning" can be presented in the vocal tones of the phrase "you will." A signed sentence with the performance verb of a promise,

PROMISE, PAY BILL NEXT-WEEK WILL

can also be interpreted, deleting the performance verb, as

"I will pay the bill next week."

By stressing the word "will," the illocutionary force of the promise is implied. A performance verb signed at the beginning of a sentence may not need to stated, because the complete meaning will be conveyed in English without it. For example, the performance verb UNDERSTAND is frequently signed at the beginning of an ASL sentence, but would rarely if ever be interpreted into English literally.

Register and Implications for Interpreters

The setting one is involved in, how fast or slow a person speaks, whether there is interaction between the speaker and listener, and the status of the people involved all have a bearing on the words people use and the style in which they present these words. Speakers of English learn that sentences need to be complete when speaking in front of a group, but know that two words spoken to a good friend carry far more meaning to that person than a casual observer can comprehend.

Language use in varying degrees of formality is referred to as "register." The concept of register helps people communicate effectively and interact in an accepted manner. Register takes into consideration the roles of the speaker and audience and what type of relationship the participants have with each other (Halliday, 1968, 1978). If register is used incorrectly, the resulting confusion in roles can cause a multitude of problems.

Language is divided into five registers, which incorporate different linguistic styles in various physical settings. Register influences how language (spoken or signed) is presented, and if the language is memorized or spontaneous (Joos, 1968). As register use becomes more formal, the relationships of the people become less personal. (Beare, 2001) The five registers are:

1. **Frozen/oratorical**: performances, public speeches, and sacred texts

2. **Formal**: presentations and introductions

3. **Consultative**: interactions at meetings, at doctor's appointments, and during classroom teaching

4. **Casual/informal**: conversations at recreational or social activities

5. **Intimate**: conversations between people who are very close to one another

Jacobson (2001) noted the five registers function as a means to analyze the way language is used. Most people are so attuned to the appropriateness of a register that they only pay attention to it when someone makes a mistake (Skrebels, 1997). When interpreting into English, an interpreter must understand how to use appropriate register, and then present the interpretation in a way that the listener would expect to hear it.

In frozen register there is a script that is followed as part of a ritual (Bar-Tzur, 2001). Every time a text is used, the same words are spoken. Examples of frozen text are the Pledge of Allegiance, the national anthem, and the Serenity Prayer. Although the participants may speak simultaneously or responsively, communication in the usual sense is not happening. Nothing new will be learned as a result of the participants speaking. The point of frozen register is to affirm that each participant is part of a larger whole.

No one is allowed to paraphrase or change the wording in these scripts. The issue for the English interpretation is that when someone signs the meaning of a frozen text, the interpreter watching the signs must look beyond the meaning conveyed by the signs and recite the frozen text into English as people listening are expecting to hear it. As a Deaf participant signs the text, the English form is of primary importance. If a Deaf person signs the Pledge of Allegiance and starts with,

```
I PROMISE SUPPORT honorific FLAG
```

the interpretation is not "I promise to support the flag," but rather "I pledge allegiance to the flag." Interpreters must keep their ears attuned to the English words that are expected by the audience. When becoming aware of the frozen text to be used, the interpreter can seek out a written form of the text, possibly from the signer or from one of the other participants. It may be necessary to read the text on paper while watching the Deaf person sign it to ensure that the correct words are used.

How the interpreter signs the frozen text to a Deaf consumer is often the way the Deaf consumer will sign it back. There are no universally accepted ASL translations for frozen English text. When the Deaf signer responds using the same signs the interpreter used, the interpreter must speak the original English frozen text. For example, a Deaf individual has been elected as an officer in an organization, and is now at the swearing-in ceremony. The person in charge says, "Do you solemnly swear to uphold the office of Secretary?" The interpreter signs, YOU PROMISE SUPPORT OFFICE SECRETARY? and the ASL user signs I PROMISE. At this point, any English speaker would say either, "I do" or "I do solemnly swear," not "I promise," and the interpreter would respond with the same words an English speaker would use.

Formal register occurs when an audience is large and there is a difference in status between speaker and audience. Deference is shown to the speaker, and participants are not expected to ask questions during the presentation (Bar-Tzur, 2001). In a formal register, there is very little participation by the listeners, as the speaker is on a dais, or somehow separated from the audience. Therefore, the audience and, most likely, the interpreter will not be able to stop and ask the speaker for clarification.

When using ASL in the formal register, the signer will communicate more slowly, articulate signs more carefully, use longer pauses, and use reiteration in which the same sign begins and ends a sentence (IRC, 1997). Any specialized vocabulary is more likely to be explained, and long pauses do not create any discomfort to the ASL user.

In a formal register, English speakers are accustomed to having the speaker speak at a slow pace, use longer words, and incorporate fewer contractions, colloquialisms, slang, or other idiomatic language (Simon & Maroney, 1997). When interpreting into English in a formal register it is critical to avoid such casual words as "gonna," "hopin'," or "kinda." This is a critical consideration as register in ASL depends more on presentation style rather than sign choice. An English speaker in this register would use a more polished and specialized vocabulary such as, "Good evening, ladies and gentlemen," rather than, "Hello, hello, hello." The interpreter aware of the language used in a particular setting, works on selecting words that give the presenter the "sound" of being formal. Employees don't "do a job"; they "perform a task." The audience may not be asked to "look at our choices" but to "explore our options."

Signers are aware that a Deaf person cannot look at something on the screen and watch someone sign at the same time, but English speakers find it uncomfortable to have long periods of silence, such as when they are looking at a slide presentation or an overhead. When the signer points to something displayed on the screen, the interpreter may want to say something like, "as you can see here in point 3B," then continue by reading it out loud.

In **consultative register**, there is a difference in status between the participants, but the difference is because one is an expert in the matter under discussion (Bar-Tzur, 2001). This register allows the listener to ask questions which will affirm the relationship among participants and their difference of status. The consultative register can be found in interactions between a teacher and student, a doctor and patient, or a lawyer and client.

A Deaf presenter in this register will communicate at a moderate pace with articulation that is not so exaggerated as in formal register, using pauses as necessary. In a classroom setting with a Deaf instructor, students will be able to ask questions during class, and the signer will check for comprehension directly with them. There will be organization in what the speaker wants to say, but there is more flexibility for a change in direction if the students show a lack of understanding or give responses that lead the teacher to take the class in a different direction.

Interpreters need to be aware of the specialized vocabulary that may be used in a presentation. A Deaf teacher may use signs that have specific English terms that are not normally seen in casual conversation, or may use more initialized signs. Knowing the specialized terms to be used ahead of time is critical so the English interpretation is not simply glossed from the signs, but rather incorporates the correct terminology for the topic. For example, a teacher may be discussing mourning and the feeling of loss when a Deaf child is born to hearing parents. One step of mourning is "denial," and the teacher may sign as ACCEPT NOT. When the teacher refers back to this step in the mourning process later in class, the English interpretation is "denial," not "doesn't accept."

In **casual register** two or more people may know each other fairly well, and the status of everyone is equal. Interpreters often see this register when they socialize and may mistakenly use this style of signing in formal and consultative settings (Bar-Tzur, 2001). The language form used in this register is sometimes referred to as "#CLUB signing."

This is the register normally used in basic ASL classes, as students would be expected to communicate with Deaf individuals on this level before being able to use the language in other registers. Casual register is actually harder to understand in ASL than the other registers because Deaf participants will sign quickly without necessarily seeking comprehension of others in the group. Some signs may also not be clearly or completely articulated.

When interpreting into this register, an interpreter can use slang and shared knowledge if he or she is able. There is a tendency in the casual register for people to overlap and interrupt each other. Situations where an interpreter may work in a casual register are wedding receptions, or if a Deaf consumer attends a conference and later sits at a table during the closing banquet with hearing colleagues.

Intimate register is talk between couples and best friends who have so much background knowledge and common experience that most outsiders would have little or no idea what is being discussed (Bar-Tzur, 2001). Interpreters may encounter this register during marriage and family counseling. When an interpreter is needed in a counseling session, maintaining one interpreter throughout the process, which could last weeks or months, will help the interpreter become familiar with intimate experiences and events that are particular to the couple or family. When a Deaf couple starts conversing directly during sessions, interpreters must feel comfortable enough to stop and ask for clarification, or tell the counselor what is being said, as much as they can understand it. The counselor will then choose how to handle these moments.

Working Within a Register

Register entails a speaker using language based on the occasion, the participants, and their relationship to one another, the topic, and the location (Zimmer, 1989; Jannedy, Poletto, & Weldon, 1994; Parker & Riley, 1994). The more experience a person has with a register, the more comfortable the person will be interpreting in that register. Many students have only their own experiences to reflect on when coming into the interpreting profession and may not have had any experience in the formal register or be familiar with it. They may also not have had formal training in giving speeches in English or ASL, or attended formal presentations in either language. To be more comfortable in the formal register, interpreting students should attend events where this register is used.

Appropriateness of style depends on the context of the communication. Interpreters must be alert to what is appropriate, as in a business setting in which the English users may address each other by name, yet the ASL user uses eye gaze. The interpreter would need to be aware of who the signer is referring to, then identify that person by name, to match what other English speakers in the meeting are doing. Also, there may be a type of greeting, a joke, or an ending to sentences that has a certain way of being expressed in a specific context that the interpreter will need to use.

Even though there are five distinct registers, features of different registers may appear in one situation, such as in a church setting where in one service participants may experience frozen, formal, and informal register.

Formulaic Elements of English

A formulaic element in a language is a specific way something is said in a particular setting. This would include such items as the greeting, "How are you?" and the response "Fine," the beginning of a presentation, "Good evening, ladies and gentlemen," or the announcement at the end of a contest, "and the winner is . . ." Zimmer (1991) notes that though frozen register is seen as the most formal speech, there are formulaic elements that occur in the most informal and casual speech.

Some stories are formulaic and frozen in concept, but not every word needs to be said exactly the same each time the story is told. However, some of the vocabulary, phrases, and sentences used in a story must follow a specific formula, and these words, phrases, and sentences enhance the story's flavor. In the fairy tale "Cinderella," the English speaker expects to hear that Cinderella had an *evil stepmother* and was rescued by a *handsome prince*. She did not have a bad step-mom, nor did a good-looking prince come and get her. The story begins "once upon a time," not "a long time ago" and "they lived happily ever after" not "from then on they were happy." The phrases used in these types of stories give people the hint that a fairy tale is being told. Interpreters doing an English interpretation of a fairy tale need to retain these words and phrases.

Summary

Illocutionary forces in English consist of the implied purpose in a sentence. In the sentence, "Mary and John are getting married" the illocutionary force is "I want to inform you." Often, in ASL the illocutionary force is stated overtly using a performance verb. The interpreter does not need to state the performance verb into English, as this information in English is usually implied and not conveyed as a separate lexical item.

The benefit to the interpreter of excluding the performance verb is being able to keep pace with the signing presenter more easily while retaining the meaning. Deleting the performance verb also produces a more idiomatic message.

Language is divided into five registers:

- **Frozen**. This register follows a script that is part of a ritual. English interpretations must use the exact English text and not merely glosses of the signs used.

- **Formal**. The audience is large, and there is a difference in status between the speaker and the audience. English interpretations should be more polished and incorporate specialized vocabulary. The interpreter should avoid casual contractions.

- **Consultative**. There is a difference of status between the participants, but the listener is in a position to ask questions. This register occurs in the classroom between teacher and students or between a doctor and patient.

- **Casual**. Two people know each other and hold equal status. Interpreters often mistakenly use this register during formal and consultative settings.

- **Intimate**. This is used between couples or best friends who share information that most outsiders are not familiar with. Interpreters would see this register during counseling.

Each register uses a different linguistic and presentation style; the relationship of the speaker and audience varies, and the physical setting is different. English interpretations must be presented in ways that are appropriate to the desired register

English has formulaic elements in which the use of frozen vocabulary, phrases, and sentences enhance a story. English users expect phrases such as "once upon a time" when hearing fairy tales. Interpreters must be aware of the language choices made in English and how certain components of language should be presented in specific contexts.

Activity 7-1

Language comparison

This exercise allows students to try to match register by taking the time to analyze a signed text before interpreting the message into English.

Step 1:

1. The teacher will select a signed presentation done in formal register.

2. Students will select a 5-minute portion of the text on which to work.

3. Students will watch the videotape and observe the signed text until they feel comfortable that they understand the portion.

Step 2:

1. While watching the tape, students will record their English interpretations on audiotape.

2. Students will present their English interpretations to the class.

3. Students will take turns playing the videotape and their audiotapes simultaneously.

4. Other students will give feedback about the English interpretation by answering the following questions:

    Was the message conveyed?
    Were English word choices equivalent to the ASL message?
    Was the register maintained?
    Was the English interpretation coherent?
    Was the English interpretation idiomatic?

Activity 7-2

In-class assignment
Frozen exercise

Step 1: Study a frozen text, such as:

The Pledge of Allegiance
Swearing someone into office
Serenity Prayer

Step 2: Students should videotape themselves or a Deaf person signing an ASL translation of the frozen text.

Step 3: Students will watch the videotape and record an English interpretation onto audiotape.

Step 4: Students will listen to the audiotape, asking themselves the following questions:

Is the English frozen text maintained?
Is the vocabulary selection correct?
Does the interpretation sound natural?
Were pauses inserted appropriately?

Activity 7-3

Discussion and group work

Many stories told in English contain formulaic idiomatic phrasing. Take the following texts and working in pairs, first underline the incorrect words and phrases and then write down the commonly used words and phrases.

The Three Little Pigs

In the past, there was a mother pig that had three mature son pigs. She felt it was time that they went out into the world to seek employment and housing. Each pig decided to build his own place to live.

The first pig built his home out of long grass. The huge, mean wolf came by and asked to be let in. The pig said, "No, I won't."

So the wolf blew really, really hard and the house fell down. The little pig went to his brother's house. The next pig had built his house out of small pieces of wood. The big, mean wolf came by and asked to be let in, but the pig and his brother said, "No, we won't."

The wolf blew and he blew and he blew, and the house collapsed. The two small pigs ran off to their brother's house. The last pig was not stupid. He built his house out of red brick. The wolf came by and told the pig to let him in, but the pig and his brothers said, "No, go away."

So the huge, bad wolf blew for a long time and the house wouldn't fall down. The wolf climbed to the top of the house and tried to go down the chimney, but the pigs were too smart for him and had a big pot of hot water at the bottom. The wolf fell down the fireplace and right into the water where he died.

Cinderella

A long time ago, in a country not near here, there lived a family whose mother died. Wanting to make sure his daughter had a mother, the father remarried, and his new wife brought in two daughters. Later, the father died. The two step-sisters were not pretty, but Cinderella was, so they were jealous and made her work and clean and cook.

One day, the good-looking prince of the nation held a party to find a future wife. All the girls with no husbands were invited. The two sisters were very excited, and planned what type of beautiful, long dresses they would wear. But Cinderella could not go. She was left home to clean.

After her step-sisters and her father's wife left, she sat down in the yard and cried. Soon a magical spirit showed up, and told her to stop crying. Because Cinderella had a good heart, she would go to the party. And with a wave of the magic stick, the magical spirit used her magic and created a carriage with horses and gave Cinderella a beautiful dress. Cinderella was thrilled, but the magical spirit said she had to be home before 12 o'clock, because that is when the magic would stop.

She went to the party, and the good-looking prince fell in love with her. When the clock pointed to 12 o'clock, Cinderella ran away, but running down the stairs, she lost her glass shoe. The prince couldn't find her, but only finding her shoe, sent out an announcement that he would look for this girl and marry her.

Arriving at Cinderella's house, the good-looking prince tried the shoe on the two half-sisters. The shoe did not fit. He tried the shoe on Cinderella, and the shoe fit. He knew he had found the right lady. The prince and Cinderella were married, and from then on they were very, very happy.

Activity 7-4

Discussion and group work

Two videotapes about register were developed by the Region X Interpreter Education Center at Western Oregon University. One deals with register variation in ASL, and the other with register variation in English. Tapes can be ordered by calling 1-800-223-5219.

Each videotape contains four language models giving two 10-minute presentations, one formal, the other informal.

Students may watch the tape and observe register variation.

Students may watch the tape and attempt to do an English interpretation that sounds formal or informal based on the register desired.

Chapter Eight

The Technology of Conversation

Interpreters can converse in ASL and in English, but when two people with different languages want to converse with each other, problems sometime occur. Communication between people does not happen in an arbitrary manner. Instead, each language employs what is called a technology of conversation (Sacks, 1984), which deals with how the exchange of information is accomplished. This technology of conversation is the give and take, the starts and stops, and all the other items that regulate everyday conversation. In the field of conversation analysis, researchers have found that the technology of conversation is different in each language, each having its own set of regulators or turn-taking systems that are used to manage conversations.

Language Regulators

Regulators for turn-taking are ways people show they are giving up a turn, wanting to take a turn to talk, or signaling the speaker to continue talking. A simple interaction involves two participants, the speaker and the listener, who will change roles when one person stops talking and the other begins. When a person is talking, he or she is producing what is called a "turn of talk" (Schegloff, 1981), which involves the collaboration of all people present in the communication process.

As bilinguals of ASL and English, interpreters are able to communicate with people in both languages without too much thought about what is needed to keep a conversation moving. When using either language, there is a "gut feeling" about when appropriate interaction is occurring and when it is not. Even though they may not be consciously aware of the rules, interpreters who are familiar with language regulators can use this knowledge to make linguistic adjustments needed to have equivalence in the two languages.

Interpreters work to make sure the two languages somehow work together and that the interaction is appropriate. To do this the interpreter becomes the director of the interaction, employing certain strategies during the interpretation and becoming an active participant (Roy, 1993). Interpreters make decisions all the time concerning which rules to follow in an interaction between a hearing and a Deaf consumer (Baker-Shenk, 1991). These rules of interaction involve which person gets to speak when two people start to talk at the same time, how people are interrupted or if an interruption even occurs, and how people keep control of their turn of talk.

Turn-Taking

Turn-taking is accomplished by how participants interact during a conversation (Sacks, Schegloff, & Jefferson, 1974). Speakers and recipients use certain mechanisms to control the flow of turn-taking, which helps listeners know when a speaker is at the beginning, in the middle, or nearing the end of a turn. These mechanisms also help recipients know when it is appropriate to start talking.

Each language has turn-taking regulators, which are ways people in each culture show they are giving up a turn, wanting to take a turn to talk, or telling the speaker to continue. ASL signers wanting to continue their turn of talk while pausing to gather their thoughts, maintain their turn by using dropped eye gaze, keeping their hands up, or holding the last sign frozen. In order to make sure a pause is not misconstrued by English speaking listeners as a cue to start talking, interpreters can use English fillers such as "hmmm," "OK," "well," or "and." If an interpreter does not use the English fillers, an English speaker may think the other person has ended the turn of talk and jump in, causing the Deaf person to lose the floor.

Any time an interpreter is working between languages, there will be pauses between speakers because of processing time. Often, English speakers using an interpreter begin a turn of talk when it is not expected because they are not used to speaking through another person. They are unaccustomed to having so much time between the end of their turn of talk and the start of the other person's turn. If there is no talking or other auditory cue, the English-speaking listener resumes the role of speaker and commences to talk again. In spoken English interaction, if the recipient does not take advantage of a chance to speak, the original speaker keeps the conversation going.

After an English speaker asks a question, a filler may be used at the beginning of the Deaf person's response in order for the Deaf person to maintain the floor. For example, the interpreter may decide to wait in order to see the whole answer signed. Because of this delay, or pause, the English speaker may ask the question again, but use different words, thinking the other person misunderstood the first time. Aware that such pauses may cause discomfort for an English speaker who is used to an immediate response, the interpreter could omit signing the second question, if it is similar to the first, and only interpret the response. Another option would be that after the question is asked, the interpreter could use a filler, such as "yes" or "well," possibly drawing it out like "weeeeellll," or a string of fillers such as "OK," short pause, "well," short pause. The use of fillers clues the questioner that the question is being answered.

Baker (1977) found that hearing counselors working with Deaf clients had difficulty in knowing when their clients were finished with a thought and were unsure when it was appropriate to respond. For counselors, the issue of timing is important in establishing rapport.

"Some people feel slighted when their last syllable is chopped by another's turn initiation. Responding too quickly may give the impression that you are not as interested in what has just been said as you are in your own reply. On the other hand, a late response is sometimes associated with lack of understanding, possible disagreement, or even disinterest, all of which make the other person uncomfortable" (p. 232).

A hearing consumer may misunderstand that a slow response time is the result of using an interpreter and not discomfort or lack of understanding from the Deaf person. Instead of thinking a long pause is a natural part of the interpreting process, the hearing consumer may feel uncomfortable during the interaction, thus making the experience of working with an interpreter and Deaf person unpleasant. Interpreters may not be able to eliminate this discomfort completely, but can be aware of it and work on ways to reduce it.

Markers

Two types of conversation regulators are "markers" and "continuers." Markers are words the speaker uses to signal what he or she plans to do during a turn of talk. Continuers are non-verbal indicators used by recipients to let a speaker know they want the speaker to continue a turn of talk. When these regulators are not interpreted properly, conflicts in Deaf-hearing interactions occur.

Sometimes speakers want to keep the floor or know they will require a relatively long turn of talk in order to get out the information needed. They use markers (Schegloff, 1981) which serve the following purposes:

First, they inform a receiver of the speaker's desire to "keep the floor" and finish the point when the other person breaks in too early. An ASL user will hold up one finger to try to maintain control of the floor or wave his hand while looking away. The interpreter would continue talking over the other person or say, "excuse me," and then continue talking.

Second, a marker is used to let the listener/recipient know the speaker plans to continue talking for a longer period of time. In English, this can be done by using a list-initiating marker, such as "first of all." This initiating marker informs the listener that after the "first" is done, there will be more information following. ASL users project they are going to list more than one item by enumeration on the non-dominant hand. By including this bit of information in the English interpretation, the interpreter informs the hearing consumer there will be more information coming. This allows the speaker to keep control of the conversation through long monologues, long descriptions, involved stories, or long responses to inquiries.

Third, a marker is used to foreshadow what a speaker plans to do during a turn of talk, such as asking a question or issuing a command. Before asking a question, a speaker may want to give some background information or make a point first. A marker used to foreshadow this is, "May I ask you a question?" (Schedgloff, 1980). Once an English speaker uses this statement, the recipient is prepared to withhold a response until the question has been asked. There are times when a question will be asked directly; other times there will be background information given first. Whether or not an explanation occurs, the person listening would wait for the question.

The signs CURIOUS or QUESTION foreshadow a question in ASL. Interpreting foreshadowing into an English marker would have the interpreter saying, "Now, let me ask you a question," or "I am wondering" or "I have a question . . ." These statements alert the English-speaking recipient that a question is going to occur. If additional information is stated first, the recipient will not interrupt and start a turn of talk, but wait for the question to be asked.

Once a question marker is stated and the person signs the question, the interpreter can interpret the question marker, then pause and wait for the complete question before interpreting it into English. The recipient, having been given a question marker, is more willing to wait through the silence because he or she knows to expect a question. This allows for an "extended turn" enabling the Deaf person to keep control of the communication.

When an interpreter does not have a clear understanding of markers and the technology of conversation, the Deaf person will usually be at a disadvantage in a conversation unless the English speaker is sensitive to Deaf culture. If not culturally sensitive, English speakers may be thrown off when the normal pace of conversation is distorted or does not fit their cultural norm. Some English speakers, unsure of what to do, handle working with an interpreter by waiting until all movement by the Deaf person stops and the interpreter's hands go down before beginning a turn of talk. This can be very awkward for the Deaf person and frustrating for the interpreter.

An interpreter often waits to begin speaking until getting a complete concept. However, in doing so, the Deaf person may lose control of the floor. This happens because, according to English conversational rules, the Deaf person appears to be not saying anything. Interpreters need to learn how to be comfortable using markers and fillers with English-speaking consumers in order to make sure the Deaf person can finish whatever he or she had planned to say.

Metzger (1999) examined neutrality in the interpretation process and noted that utterances generated by the interpreter which were not part of the source language are still necessary. Metzger states:

> If interpreters add no interpreter-generated contributions to the interaction, certain information that is normally accessible in interactive discourse would be missing. If equivalency is supposed to be a marker of neutrality, certainly the omission of this type of information would detract from neutrality. Thus, an interpreter's offering 'extra' information or utterances in order to provide equal information actually minimizes the interpreter's influence on the interaction (p. 157).

This "extra" information includes the markers needed to keep a conversation moving. ASL users not wanting to give up the floor in the middle of a turn of talk may:

Keep hands up, not returning to the rest position.

Fill pauses with movements that show thinking, such as looking up, shifting posture, or furrowing the brow.

Hold the last sign.

Shift eye gaze away to get their thoughts together before continuing.

English speakers keep control of their turn of talk by (Schegloff, 1981):

Adding signals such as "OK" or "um" or "and."

Not acknowledging the other person while continuing to talk.

Speeding up the pace of talk, continuing to talk when approaching the end of a unit and not taking a breath until they are into their next unit of talk.

Interpreters, aware that a Deaf consumer is not ready or willing to lose a turn of talk, would take the visual information from the signer and present it in a way an English speaker would understand by using any of the examples mentioned above.

Continuers

Recipients, or listeners, show speakers they want them to go on with their turn of talk without interruption by the use of continuers, which serve several major purposes (Schegloff, 1981). They enable recipients to show the speaker that they are:

Paying attention.

Wanting the speaker to continue.

Understanding what is being said.

Agreeing with what is being said.

English uses continuers such as "uh huh," "mm hmmm" and words such as "yeah," "I see," "good," "oh" and "OK." Continuers in ASL consist of the use of non-manual markers such as raised eyebrows, head nods, or a MMM facial expression. Signs used as continuers are "OH-I-SEE," "RIGHT," "REALLY," or "UNDERSTAND." These are also called feedback or back-channeling signals.

In order for the intent of non-manual markers to be completely understood by an English speaker, an interpreter must vocalize an equivalent at the appropriate time, either verbally or non-verbally. This vocalization ensures that the English speaker feels that the Deaf recipient is involved fully in the interaction. Anyone who thinks these continuers are not important should try to remember a time when there was no response to some spoken discourse with another person. An English user would be unsure what to do if the Deaf person gave no reaction to what was being said.

Continuers are often not interpreted because many interpreters think they have no semantic significance and do not contribute to the substance of the discourse. However, continuers do have semantic value. In interactive settings, they allow the speaker to know the recipients are involved in the conversation and help the communication process continue.

One difficulty for the interpreter is in signing the English text while at the same time vocalizing the ASL continuers. This is not as difficult as it seems. If the Deaf consumer gives appropriate non-manual feedback, the interpreter can scatter this feedback throughout the signed interpretation. Occasionally saying "uh huh" while signing may be all that is needed for the English speaker to feel that the Deaf person is involved. This takes practice, but it can be done.

Claiming a Turn of Talk

Another area to examine is how a Deaf person signals wanting to claim a turn of talk. This is done by:

Increasing head nodding in size and frequency, comparable to an English user saying OK a lot more.

Raising the palm.

Changing from a rest position to pointing, touching, or waving the hand in front of the speaker.

Switching eye gaze or posture.

Interrupting and repeating the first few signs.

People attuned to a visual-gestural language understand these non-manual markers, but English users, who depend almost exclusively on auditory cues, are frequently unaware of them. Therefore, an interpreter must remember to give auditory cues when a Deaf person wants to claim a turn of talk.

English speakers indicate a desire to talk by producing the sound "uh huh" or "right," before starting their turn, or by repeating the word "OK" more often than before. When seeing the marker of the continual head nod by the ASL user, the interpreter would start using the English words "OK," pause, "OK," or "uh huh, uh huh."

Ending a Turn of Talk

When a person is ready to end a turn of talk, each language employs different techniques. When ASL users are ready to stop talking, they will (Baker 1977):

Return to direct eye gaze.

Decrease signing speed (optional).

Index the receiver (optional).

Return their hands to a rest position.

English speakers ending a turn of talk will lower the voice, say the word "OK," or leave a long pause, allowing the other person to become the speaker. The English interpretation of any of the ASL options could be to simply say "OK."

Summary

There is often a "gut feeling" about when appropriate interaction is occurring in a given language. When working between two languages, however, interpreters must be overtly aware of how people in both languages accomplish certain tasks. The more they understand the rules of interaction, the better the interpretation will be.

Because English speakers are not attuned to the visual cues that Deaf individuals give, these visual cues need to have auditory equivalents. Speakers may at times project, with a use of markers, their desire to take a longer turn of talk or to foreshadow a communicative task such as asking a question. Before asking a question an English speaker might say, "I have a question." ASL users might sign CURIOUS or QUESTION. The interpreter could say "I'm curious," but being aware that this is a marker for a question, might better state, "I have a question" or "I'm wondering."

There are times the recipient wants the speaker to know he or she is in agreement, or wants the speaker to go on, but does not want to interrupt. To do this, English speakers use continuers such as "uh huh," or "hmmm," or the words "yeah," "I see" or "OK." ASL users will use head nods, or raise or lower the eyebrows. Signs used are OH, RIGHT, and UNDERSTAND. These ASL continuers need to be interpreted so the English speaker knows communication is occurring.

Interpreters must remember that English speakers, like ASL users, have a strong sense of what is expected during a conversation. The more an interpreter is attuned to the auditory needs of the recipient, the smoother the interpretation will be.

Activity 8-1

Turn-taking exercise

Step 1: The class will be divided into groups as small as four people but no larger than six people. Each person will discuss his or her plans for the upcoming weekend with one person working as a monitor.

Step 2: Each person must ask the group at least one question to which each member will respond. A sample question might be, "Who will you go with?"

Restriction

Once a person has stopped talking, no one in the group may respond for three seconds. The monitor in each group will ensure that this restriction is followed.

Step 3: Groups will continue this exercise for 5 minutes.

Step 4: At the end of five minutes, group members will answer the following questions:

What was the most difficult aspect about this exercise?

What feelings were experienced during the three-second wait?

How might hearing consumers would react to a three-second pause?

Step 5: Responses will be shared with the whole class.

Activity 8-2

Turn-taking exercise
English out of class assignment

Listen to a conversation in which two people are speaking English.

Mark down any time speakers use such words as: "uh huh," "yeah," "I see," "really," "oh," and "OK."

Write down if the words were used to:

Start a turn of talk

End a turn of talk

Show the speaker the recipient is listening

Try to take over a turn of talk

End the conversation

Activity 8-3

Turn-taking exercise
ASL out of class assignment

Watch a conversation in which two people are signing.

Mark down any time a speaker uses signs such as "UNDERSTAND," "OH-I-SEE," "REALLY," or a head nod.

Write down if these features were used to:

Start a turn of talk

End a turn of talk

Show the speaker the recipient is listening

Try to take over a turn of talk

End the conversation

Chapter Nine

Transition Markers

Transition markers are linguistic features used to help determine how the elements of one utterance are related to another (Humphries, 2000). All languages use transition markers to show when there is a shift from old information to new information, or when a speaker is moving on to a new topic. Transition markers can also be thought of as connecting words or signs that hold the discourse together.

Importance of Transition Markers

As a person talks, or signs, an interpreter keeps the relationship between the topic and subsequent comments in mind. When a topic changes, the comments thereafter are related to the new topic. Discourse often consists of one topic or a series of topics followed by commentary, which supports or supplements the main topic (Larson, 1998).

Transition markers used to signal a change in topic in ASL include the signs WELL, HAPPEN, FINISH, INFORM YOU, KNOW-THAT, NOW, ANYWAY, UNDERSTAND, FINE. BUT, and #SO. In English, transition markers include pauses and such words as: "OK," "fine," "now," "so," "and," "well," "likewise," "however," "although," "for example," "therefore," "consequently," "because," "since," "first," "next," and "subsequently" (Humphries, 2000).

Without transition markers in an interpretation, the English-speaking audience hears only isolated details and is unaware of how the chunks of information relate to one another. These markers help guide the listener to have a clear understanding of the overall picture of what is being said. They are incorporated throughout the discourse to help the listener discern how sentences relate and how one comment is connected to another. They also help the listener know when a particular topic ends and a new one begins.

Issues an interpreter should consider during an English interpretation are as follows:

How does the current point or topic relate to the previous point or topic?

Is the information being presented a comparison, a contrast, an example, a segue ,or an aside?

What transition word(s) would clarify this relationship?

When a speaker does not clearly state the goal or objective of the discourse, the interpreter must try to formulate a framework within which to work. By doing this, the interpreter can make appropriate word choices in the English interpretation.

For example, in the videotape"Comparing ASL and English Features: Implications for Voice Interpreting," a Deaf woman is relating the activities surrounding her 10-year high school reunion. She was on the committee for the event and shares during the beginning of her talk about all of the work she did to get ready for the night of the reunion. She then describes setting up the tables and getting the room ready. Finally, she introduces the topic of her classmates arriving. This last portion is introduced in the following manner:

> TABLE PUT PUT CL:CC READY (slight head nod) CL:I (come towards signer, alternate hands, 4 times) WOW HUG HUG SEE LONG-TIME WOW (the signer then goes on to describe what has happened to the people since she last saw them.)

The English interpretation must make it clear that the reunion has begun:

> "The room was ready and people started arriving. I greeted people I hadn't seen in a long time."

A skewed interpretation would be:

> "The tables were ready and people came up to me, I hugged them."

By the expression on her face and pauses used in the signing, the topic that the reunion has begun is marked, so the people greeting her must be her classmates although she never overtly signs that they are. In the first interpretation, the English-speaking consumer gets a sense that her fellow classmates have arrived. In the second example, there could be a misunderstanding of who the people are coming up to her. They could have been from the hotel.

Transition Markers in ASL

An example of a transition marker occurs in the following example from a description of a camping trip:

> NIGHT COOK FOOD, UNDERSTAND DRY FOOD TASTE AWFUL. BUT MUST EAT. STOMACH BARK NEED FOOD, ANYWAY ATE FINISH SIT RELAX TELL STORY

The word ANYWAY alerts the listener that the topic of needing to eat, even if the food tastes bad, has ended. The signs following ANYWAY comprise the next topic. An English interpretation could be:

> "That night we cooked our food. It was dry and tasted awful, but we had to eat; we were hungry. So, we ate anyway and then sat around and told stories."

A problem arises when a transition marker is not recognized correctly, causing the subsequent information to remain connected to the previous topic. In the example above, if the interpreter says "doesn't matter" for ANYWAY, the statement will imply that all the information said prior to this point was not important, rather than marking the next sentence as a new topic. As a topic marker, ANYWAY can be interpreted into English as either a clear ending of the previous sentence or as a pause before starting the next sentence with "so."

The signed transition marker INFORM-YOU, coupled with the signer leaning the body to the side, signals an aside in the narrative and should be treated as such in the English interpretation. Once the aside is finished, the signer resumes an upright stance and continues with the story. The interpretation of INFORM-YOU should not be literal. Instead of saying, "I need to inform you," which may be too formal in a story setting, one could say, "by the way," and drop the pitch of the voice.

Another sign used to introduce a topic in ASL is NOW. This sign, instead of functioning as a temporal marker, sometimes signals that a new topic is about to begin. The sign KNOW-THAT is also used as an introduction of a new topic.

When ending a topic, before moving on to the next one, ASL users will pause, give a slight head nod, clasp their hands, or perhaps drop their hands. Signs that indicate a topic has ended are ANYWAY, PUSH-ASIDE, NEXT or enumerating and moving to a new finger. A signal of topic change must be stated in English. Words that move the English listener to a new topic are "now," "ok," "next," "then," or "so."

A new topic may be handled by the interpreter clearly stating the last sentence, pausing, and then beginning the next sentence as a statement. The information that follows will pertain to the new topic because pauses are a way for English speakers to move on to a new topic.

The word "and" does not differentiate topics, but rather, implies more information will be given about the previous topic. In English, speakers end a topic by simply ending a sentence. If an interpreter misuses the word "and," a discourse containing different topics will sound odd. One such example is:

> I grew up in southern California, and grew up in a family with two sisters, and we loved to go to Disneyland every year, and later I got married, and my husband had never gone to Disneyland with his family, and he did not have the same childhood memories of the place, and he did not want to go with me the first year we were married, and I got mad, and after having children I wanted to go to Disneyland, and I asked him to come just one time, and he did, and can you believe it, he really loved it, and now he wants to take our two girls back next year.

Instead of using "and," the interpreter could be aware of sentence boundaries or use English words that clearly mark a new topic. The result is a story that flows better:

> I grew up in southern California in a family with two sisters. We loved to go to Disneyland every year (pause).

> Later, I married, and my husband had never gone to Disneyland with his family and did not have the same childhood memories of the place. He did not want to go there with me the first year we were married, and I got mad (pause).

> After we had children, I wanted to go to Disneyland with the kids, but he didn't. I asked him to come just one time, and he did. Can you believe it? He really loved it. Now he wants to take our two girls back next year.

In most presentations there will be subtopics that fall under the main subject. Some topics may have only one or two supporting sentences, while others may have paragraphs that support and explain them. In one example of a signed story about a husband and wife owning a RV, the topics include:

The narrator telling of his early years camping with his family and his adventures across the country.

His marrying a woman who did not like to camp and how they decided to resolve this difference.

Their experiences of renting an RV.

The purchase of the RV and how the interior was set up.

Some comments about the two of them and their family traveling in the RV.

Some sections were longer than others; some topics lasted one sentence, others lasted 20 sentences, but at the end of each topic there was a pause and a head nod.

Conjunctions

Conjunctions are words that link words, phrases, clauses, sentences, or paragraphs. English contains many conjunctions (Larson, 1998), both coordinate and subordinate. ASL also has conjunctions. Some signs that serve as conjunctions in ASL are WRONG, HAPPEN, HIT, and FRUSTRATE (Humphries, Padden, & O'Rourke, 1980). These signs do not always serve as conjunctions, but, as such, they should not be interpreted according to their primary meaning. Instead they should take on the form of a conjunction in English.

The sign WRONG, with a twisting movement on the chin, means "without warning" or "suddenly." For example, a girl inside a house wants to go outside, but runs into a sliding glass door. This is because she didn't notice the door was closed.

GIRL WALK NORMAL, FAST NOT, WALK GLASS DOOR WRONG HIT-WALL FALL DOWN

English: She was just walking when suddenly she hit the glass door and fell down.

The sign WRONG does not usually mean "accidentally." There is a need for a word that shows a relationship between the girl walking and then hitting the door. This idea does not come across by saying the word "wrong." Other English words or phrases that could replace WRONG in this context are "unexpectedly," "all of a sudden," "without warning," or "abruptly."

When HAPPEN is used as a conjunction, it can mean "just so happened that."

MY FRIEND, ME WANT SEE. LATER ME GO-TO STORE, HAPPEN MEET.

English: I wanted to see my friend, and it just so happened that I met her at the store.

The sign HAPPEN can also be interpreted as "when."

HAPPEN I-GO SCHOOL

English: When I go to school.

HAPPEN can also show a relationship between sentences or clauses.

SISTER NEED DRESS GO-TO STORE HAPPEN S-A-L-E

English: My sister needed a dress, and the store she went to just happened to be having a sale.

Not: My sister needed a dress and went to the store. It happened the store was having a sale.

Notice the difference between the two interpretations. The first one is a complete thought; the second one leaves the listener waiting for more information. Another example is:

ME BUY NEW CAR FRIDAY. HAPPEN MONDAY STOLE

English: I bought a new car on Friday, and then it was stolen on Monday.

The "and then" is the conjunction that connects the two thoughts in English the same way the sign HAPPEN connects the two thoughts in ASL.

The sign HIT, when used as a conjunction, means that something happened unexpectedly, or "turned out that." The sign HIT indicates that the clause before it conveys what might be expected, but the clause following HIT conveys what was not expected. In the next example, a person is saying she needed to talk with her sister, but could not reach her by TTY. She decided to go to the grocery store and planned to call her sister later.

I GO-TO FOOD STORE HIT SISTER THERE

English: I went to the grocery store, and, can you believe it, I ran into my sister there.

The idiomatic phrasing of "ran into" also implies an event that was unplanned; the two met by chance. The following example is from Humphries (1980):

SHE RESEARCH A-S-L, HIT FIND RULE RULE

English: She was doing research on ASL, and it turned out that she discovered many rules.

Not: She was doing research on ASL. She found many rules.

The "it turned out" guides the listener in recognizing that the rules were discovered while she was doing the research. Other English words that could serve as equivalents of the HIT conjunction would be "suddenly," "by surprise," "unforeseen," and "unanticipated."

The conjunction FRUSTRATE is used after a statement of something the signer had hoped to be, do, or get, but was later to be prevented from.

SUNDAY I DROVE STORE, FRUSTRATE BUSINESS SHUT-DOWN

English: Sunday I went to the store only to find out it was out of business.

Other English equivalents for FRUSTRATE could be "disappointed," "annoyed," or "saddened." As seen in the examples above, sometimes the meaning in a one-sign conjunction requires several words in English to convey the meaning.

The Word OK

English and ASL both use the word "OK," but each language uses it in different ways and for different purposes. Participants in an English conversation rely heavily on the word "OK" to keep a conversation going. In ASL there may be another sign or a non-manual signal used to represent the concept or function of the word "OK" in English. Beach (1993) has outlined the different purposes "OK" fills in English:

1. "OK" is used in a dialogue as a response to what was said by the other person before taking one's own turn of talk. When one person is talking, the listener may say "OK, I see your point, but I think . . ." This use of "OK" allows the listener to jump in and become the speaker.

    ASL users do not usually sign OK to take over a turn of talk, but would use a more vigorous head nod. Noting the head nod, the interpreter should say "OK" or some equivalent such as "yeah" at the beginning of the Deaf person's turn to let the English consumer know the Deaf person is planning to take a turn.

2. "OK" is used to show understanding of what was said previously.

    A: Your mother wants you.

    B: OK.

    In English, "OK" here does not mean that the person is going to do anything about the information received, but simply that the person understands what was said. ASL users who understand what was said may sign FINE. The interpreter could say "fine" or "OK."

3. "OK" is used as an affirmative answer to a question.

    A: Can I borrow your car this afternoon?

    B: OK.

    In this instance, the English user means "yes" when saying "OK." When an ASL user signs YES or SURE or OK, the interpreter has the option to say either "yes," "sure," or "OK."

4.　"OK" is used to show confirmation and agreement with what was said during the previous turn of talk.

　　A: You'll be here about eight?

　　B: Yes.

　　A: OK.

　　An ASL user might sign GOOD to show confirmation of what has just been signed. The interpreter can say "OK" in the English interpretation.

5.　"OK" is used in pre-closings and closings of a conversation. English speakers will notice the increase of the word "OK" before a conversation ends. This device is used to either initiate movement toward closure of a topic, terminate a phone call, or conclude an interactive situation. Listeners can also cue a speaker that they wish the conversation to end by a repeated use of "OK."

　　When ASL users indicate they wish a conversation to end by signing FINISH, the English interpretation in a one-on-one interaction could be to say the word "OK" more often, or once, emphatically.

6.　"OK" is used as an attempt to gain the floor, or to get or keep the floor. ASL users raise a hand, palm out, or begin nodding more, body moving forward. The interpreter could interpret these movements by saying "OK" more often.

7.　"OK" is used by a group leader in order to close proceedings or to finish one topic before moving on to a new one. ASL users could sign ANYWAY, NOW, NEXT, have a slight head nod, or use the "push away to the side" sign to close a topic and move on to a new one. Interpreters could say "OK" for any of these ASL transition markers.

When interpreting into English, a number of signs may have their equivalent meaning in the word "OK."

Summary

Transition markers help to relate elements of discourse to one another. An interpreter keeps these relationships in mind when doing an English interpretation to ensure that all the parts of the discourse fit together in an understandable fashion.

During an English interpretation, an interpreter should think about these questions:

　　How does this point relate to the last?

　　Is the information a comparison, a contrast, an example, a segue, or an aside?

　　What transition word would clarify this relationship?

Conjunctions are words used to join together words, phrases, clauses, sentences or paragraphs. Many ASL conjunctions, such as WRONG, HAPPEN, HIT, and FRUSTRATE, should not be interpreted according to their primary meanings when serving as conjunctions.

The word "OK" serves seven different purposes in English, which may or may not have the word "OK" as the best equivalent in ASL. If an ASL user produces a sign that is not signed as OK, the English equivalent could still be the word "OK."

Activity 9-1

Transition markers

Class work

Step 1: Watch a 5- to 10-minute signed monologue.

Step 2: Write down all the transition markers that are used, such as, WELL, HAPPEN, FINISH, INFORM-YOU, KNOW-THAT, NOW, ANYWAY, UNDERSTAND, FINE, BUT, and #SO.

Note if they start or end a topic in ASL and write the English word or words that would best convey the meaning of each.

TM   Ends topic   Starts topic   English

Activity 9-2

Conjunction functions

Step 1: Watch a 5- to 10-minute conversation in which two people are signing.

Step 2: Mark down any time a speaker uses a conjunction sign. These would include WRONG, HIT, HAPPEN, or FRUSTRATE.

Step 3: Write the English word that best conveys the meaning of each.

ASL conjunction   English interpretation

Chapter Ten

How to Improve an
ASL-to-English Interpretation

The task of interpretation is both an art and a science. For this reason, interpreters should not assume that there is only one right way to interpret a unit of meaning. Language is fluid; there are many ways to express the same meaning using different words each time.

While interpreting from ASL to English, the two main questions to keep in mind are:

1. Was the meaning intended by the Deaf consumer conveyed?

2. Was English used in such a way that the hearing consumer understood it clearly?

It is interesting how some interpreters seem to be more concerned about whether they got the individual words right, rather than having the overall message make sense. Knowing what the signs mean is just the beginning of understanding and producing the entire message. In addition, the interpretation must sound natural and follow the grammatical rules of the target language.

Along with conveying the message accurately, interpreters need to also take on the characteristics and persona of the persons for whom they are interpreting, both in ASL to English and English to ASL. The persona is often described as a character in a dramatic or literary work, or the role a person assumes to display his conscious intentions to himself and others (Morris, 1980). Like actors in a play, interpreters "take on" the persona of the Deaf consumer. This concept of persona involves much more than just the speaking of the words; it affects how the entire message is presented.

Improving English Skills

Sometimes interpreters get nervous before interpreting into English. This is normal, but they can work on different ways to be prepared. First, good English skills are a must. Frishberg (1997) believes that weakness in spoken language skill is a possible reason for difficulty in providing a good ASL-to-English interpretation. Seleskovitch (1978) believes "in order to learn how to interpret, the would-be interpreter must already have acquired a command of his language" (p. 77). Monikowski (1994) believes that "students entering an interpreter education program should demonstrate a high level of proficiency in their L1 and L2" (p. 32). So just learning more signs and working on ASL skill building is not enough to improve ASL-to-English interpreting.

Increasing vocabulary. The average person's vocabulary ranges from 3,000 to 12,000 words (Waldhorn, 1981). If a person reads extensively, word recognition may exceed 50,000 words. An average person has two types of vocabulary, passive and active (Dickerson, 1991). Passive vocabulary, the more extensive of the two, is made up of words a person can recognize when reading or listening but would not tend to use when speaking. A person's active vocabulary consists of words used when talking with others.

Shuey (2001) states that interpreters also have a "hot seat" vocabulary, which incorporates all the words the interpreter can access while interpreting. This "hot seat" vocabulary is usually even smaller than a person's active vocabulary. She recommends that in order to increase the "hot seat" vocabulary, interpreters must increase both their active and passive vocabulary. Even though English may be someone's native language, vocabulary acquisition is beneficial, and there are many ways to accomplish this task.

Keeping a vocabulary notebook. Interpreters must be aware of how the English language is used. They can note different ways the same concept is said or new ways of presenting information. Word usage will always change. Terms such as "24/7" and "peachy keen" may appear and disappear from everyday language. If interpreters are open to increasing English vocabulary, they will be surprised at how many words they have not noticed before. It is helpful to keep a notebook that would include words both heard and read. Discussing these words or phrases with other interpreters is also a way to acquire a larger English vocabulary.

Keeping a grammar notebook. Interpreters need to listen to how English speakers really use the language. They should listen to how teenagers or older people convey ideas, or how an idea is presented in different registers, rhythms, and combinations of words, looking for idiomatic phrasing in English. Jotting down English expressions in a notebook is very useful. Later, a person could look at this notebook and try to plan which words or phrases would be used to represent the meaning of a particular sign or combination of signs.

Monitoring the use of one's own English. Interpreters should pay attention to how stories are started, people are greeted, and information is presented in everyday English, not just while interpreting. Taking a public speaking course can increase one's knowledge and skill of how to speak in front of people. Being overtly aware of how English is used makes it easier to work between the languages.

Falling in love with English. Interpreters should try to analyze why certain words are used in an ad, a story, or a song. They can look words up in the dictionary and discover the nuances of the language. They can ask questions, such as, "Is there a difference between the words 'spirit' and 'soul' and what is the difference?" They can also discover the origins of words.

Working on English interpretations from pictures or stories without words. Frishberg (1997) suggests that interpreters practice using silent or wordless videos as source materials. The video "The Red Balloon" or cartoons that use no words, such as "Roadrunner" or "Tom and Jerry," can help interpreters work on English-speaking skills without worrying about going between two languages.

The next step would be to watch a short, signed monologue. Once the complete message is understood, an outline of the story can be created. From the outline, an English interpretation can be prepared, taking time to focus on making sure tense is correct, all pronouns are present, and the story flows. When the written text is completed, the interpretation can be recorded and played back, noting areas that need improvement and those done well.

Presenting a Clear Vocal Message

Interpreters need to understand the components that make up the ability to speak. When these components are recognized and understood, there is better control over the output of the English message. Vassallo (1990) says the voice is the tool used to convey the message that one is interested in getting across to the recipient. Using the voice to the best of its ability requires understanding that it is much like an instrument that must be practiced in order to get the most out of it.

Interpreters need to become familiar with and recognize how their own voices sound. Many people do not like the sound of their own voice, but unless interpreters take the time to hear themselves and analyze their own voices, they will be unable to recognize the strengths and weaknesses they bring to interpreting into spoken English.

If someone's voice is high-pitched, that person would do well to try to lower it. This is accomplished by relaxing the throat muscles, because tense muscles create an artificially high vocal pitch. Those with a high-pitched voice need to train their ears to find the proper vocal pitch. Many community colleges have voice and diction classes under the speech communication department geared toward helping people work on pronunciation, enunciation, and vocal quality. Drama departments in colleges and universities typically offer classes in voice and diction that can be taken in order to learn how to use the voice effectively.

A nasal tone may be caused by a tight jaw or tension in the muscles in the back of the tongue. This problem can be lessened or eliminated by opening the mouth and keeping the lower jaw as relaxed as possible when speaking.

Because ASL can be presented in very colorful and expressive ways, interpreters should not fall into the habit of always interpreting in a monotone. If this is a problem, one can practice by reading a written text with different emotions in it, paying special attention to voice modulation. Varma (2002) conducted a study on how the interpreter's voice impacts the credibility level of those listening. The study focused on "expressive" and "monotone" voices, and concluded that expressive voices scored higher in credibility. The signer's credibility was perceived as weaker when the interpreter's voice was monotonous. To develop an expressive voice, Varma suggests that instead of trying to sound like one would imagine the speaker would, an interpreter should use his or her own voice, taking the information given through the signed message and presenting it in a manner that is natural to the interpreter.

In order to do this, interpreters need to learn how they sound in different settings, such as formal lectures, classroom presentations, job interviews, work meetings, and one-on-one interactions. If interpreters have had no personal experience talking for themselves in these areas, it would help to get training and experience. Speech classes help people learn how to get up in front of a group of people and make a point. The Optimist Club gives people opportunities to learn to speak on many subjects. The point is, interpreters must know their own "voice" before they can accurately convey the "voice" of another person.

Two principal factors comprising a spoken message are the verbal and the vocal (Miller, 1972). The verbal includes the words spoken. The vocal includes the rate of speech, volume, and inflection. An interpreter must take the words and emotions conveyed by an ASL presenter and include both aspects in the spoken interpretation. Effective communication depends on the blending of these two areas.

Interpreters need to maintain consistent volume, especially when artificial amplification is not provided. Smaller settings, such as classrooms or staff meetings rarely have microphones available. In addition, ASL-to-English interpreters often face the front of a room, away from the listening audience. What may seem loud to the interpreter in this situation will seem normal to the people sitting right behind, since the voice must carry to the front wall and bounce backwards to reach the audience.

Interpreting into English requires clear enunciation. The audience needs to hear each word since most people will not understand any of the signs being used; the words the interpreter uses are the only source for information. One of the most common mistakes is not properly enunciating the final sounds of words (Vassallo, 1990), especially words such as "going," not "gonna," "don't you," not "doncha," and "have to," not "hafta."

Interpreters should be aware of pronunciation used in their community or region. When interpreting for a Deaf Texan, the term "y'all" would be appropriate, but while interpreting for a Deaf individual from Southern California during a national conference, an interpreter would not say "y'all," but rather "all of you."

Another consideration interpreters need to keep in mind is to avoid adding words that do not add to the message, such as "y'know" or "like," or fillers such as "umm," "uh" or "er" when not serving the purpose of holding the floor. Just as bad is the interpreter adding words that don't add to the interpretation, such as the word "well." Or the situation of an interpreter deciding to use sentence fragments and never clearly ending a sentence. When this happens, the hearing consumer will have difficulty recognizing where one point ends and another begins. Sentences need to be complete, make sense, and be connected cohesively throughout a presentation.

Adding fillers, using the word "and," never taking a breath, or not pausing between concepts or topics may happen if the interpreter feels there should never be silence or breaks in the English interpretation. However, there are times when it is appropriate or even necessary to be silent. Silence enhances English speech; if a pause is used appropriately, the listener is willing to wait for the message to continue. Listeners also need time to process information they are receiving. Pauses inherent in spontaneous speech allow listeners to think about, incorporate, and connect what is being said. Silence helps the listener know the Deaf person has come to the end of a thought or a topic, and also allows the interpreter to catch his or her breath.

Improving Presentation Skills

Being well prepared. Knowing the topic ahead of time enables the interpreter to research relevant information and become aware of any pertinent or specialized vocabulary related to that subject. Interpreters can practice saying aloud the names of speakers, organizations, or acronyms that will be used in the presentation. When possible, the interpreter should obtain a copy of the presentation or at least an outline. The more known about a subject, the better the interpretation will be.

Taking deep breaths. Someone who is nervous tends to run out of breath. Breathing deeply breaks this cycle and has a calming effect (Vassallo, 1990). Many interpreters have a card they carry around with them, with one word in bold letters, "BREATHE." Before interpreting, taking several slow, deep breaths can help an interpreter become composed.

Picturing success. Interpreters should imagine themselves doing a good job. This would include envisioning themselves forming complete sentences, having the audience understand the interpretation, and having the Deaf consumer confident with their abilities. An attitude of doing one's best and providing consumers with the best job possible goes a long way in improving performance.

Avoiding negativity. Interpreters should not think, "I can't do this," or "I never catch the fingerspelling." Thinking negatively just increases the jitters, and when an error occurs, a downward spiral begins that is difficult to escape. Instead of negative self-talk, one should make positive affirmations such as, "I can do this," or "I will understand the message and make a clear interpretation."

Handling errors. No interpreter will be able to do a job that is 100% perfect. Even speakers who have everything written down can still miss something. Dwelling on a mistake is distracting and takes energy away from the task at hand. The best advice sometimes is to keep on going. Interpreters who have made an error need to stop, collect themselves, and then pick up from where the error occurred and move on.

Not apologizing. An interpreter may want to apologize for what appears to be a mistake. If the mistake is obvious, the audience will notice it, and apologizing will not make it go away. However, if the audience did not notice it, if the mistake was later repaired, or if the mistake did not skew the message, there is no need to say anything. Apologies not only erode the interpreter's confidence; they also cause the audience to lose faith in the interpretation.

While interpreting into English, the only time to offer an apology is when an error cannot be corrected in the midst of the interpretation. If this were to happen, the best thing to do is to stop the presenter and let him or her know what happened. Either the consumer will clear the error up, or the interpreter can fix it at that point. Preconferencing with consumers on how to handle such situations is crucial.

Skill Development

Once an interpreter has mastered some of the components of Sign-to-English interpreting, there is a need to ensure that skill development will continue. No matter how good an interpreter becomes, he or she can always improve. The idea behind life-long learning is that a person is always in the state of becoming, always striving but never arriving (Kelly, 1998). Learning to improve Sign-to-English interpreting requires life-long learning, yet learning means change, and sometimes people are uncomfortable with change because they are unsure of what to expect.

A person beginning to learn enters into what is called a cycle of learning, which contains four different levels (O'Connor & Seymour, 1990):

Unconscious incompetence

Conscious incompetence

Conscious competence

Unconscious competence

Unconscious incompetence means a person is not aware of the areas of skill needing improvement. A study done by Kruger and Dunning (1999) focused on how people used knowledge. The author states that when people are incompetent, they suffer a dual burden. First, they reach erroneous conclusions about their ability to perform and make unfortunate choices. Then, because they are incompetent, they do not have the ability to even realize they are incompetent. In fact, people who are incompetent are left with the mistaken impression that what they are doing is fine. The study went on to make four predictions about people who are incompetent in a particular area (p. 1125).

Prediction 1. Incompetent individuals, compared with their more competent peers, will dramatically overestimate their ability and performance relative to objective criteria.

Prediction 2. Incompetent individuals will suffer from deficient metacognitive skills, in that they will be less able than their more competent peers to recognize competence when they see it, be it their own or anyone else's.

Prediction 3. Incompetent individuals will be less able than their more competent peers to gain insight into their true level of performance by means of social comparison information. In particular, because of their difficulty recognizing competence in others, incompetent individuals will be unable to use information about the choices and performances of others to form more accurate impressions of their own abilities.

Prediction 4. Incompetent people can gain insight about shortcomings, but this comes, paradoxically, by making them more competent, thus providing them the metacognitive skills necessary to be able to realize that they have performed poorly.

For these reasons, interpreters need to put themselves into situations that will reveal areas which need improving. This can be done by joining a study group, working with a mentor, or attending workshops. As they open themselves up to improvement, they become aware of any lack of proficiency, which moves them to the next level, conscious incompetence.

Conscious incompetence is achieved when learners become aware of areas needing improvement. Entering this level of learning becomes very uncomfortable, frustrating, and difficult. While working on developing a new skill, errors will be made, and the learner is acutely aware of them. At this level, some people revert back to old ways of doing things with the belief they were better off before they knew what they had to fix. This level takes determination and the recognition that all the hard work will pay off with better skills. This is the stage in which a person learns the most.

The next level is conscious competence. At this level, a new skill has been learned but not mastered. The skill still requires some effort to perform it correctly. At this stage, interpreters will notice improvement, which will lead them to the last stage of learning, unconscious competence.

Unconscious competence means a skill has been performed and worked on long enough to have become an ingrained habit, which then becomes an unconscious skill. While a new competence becomes unconscious, life-long learners open themselves up again to more learning and soon become aware of other incompetencies. At this point, the learning cycle begins again, as the interpreter tackles another problem area.

Personality Traits and Skill Development

Personality type will affect how someone approaches skill development. Gordon (1999) stated that personality traits can affect a person's ability to do a job. One such trait is whether a person is an internalizer or an externalizer. Internalizers feel they can control their own actions. Externalizers believe others control their lives. A person can decide which they are by answering the following ten questions taken from Aero and Weiner (1981):

1. Do you believe that if somebody studies hard, he or she can pass any subject?

2. Do you feel that you have a considerable amount of choice in deciding who your friends are?

3. Do you believe that whether or not people like you depends on how you act?

4. Do you feel that when good things happen, they happen because of hard work?

5. Do you think it's better to be smart than to be lucky?

6. Do you believe that most problems will solve themselves if you just don't fool with them?

7. Are some people just born lucky?

8. Are you most often blamed for things that just aren't your fault?

9. Do you feel that most of the time it doesn't pay to try hard because things never turn out right anyway?

10. Do you believe that wishing can make good things happen?

Answering "yes" to questions 1-5, indicates an internalizer. Answering "yes" to questions 6-10, indicates an externalizer.

Internalizers believe they can control their ability to improve skills themselves, and may do well with planning how to go about this. They may be able to find out information on their own by simply going to workshops and reading.

Externalizers are more dependent on someone else to give them guidance. They will need more of a hands-on mentor who will do a lot of follow up and tell them exactly what they need to improve their skills. Regardless of whether someone is an internalizer or an externalizer, skill-building requires goals.

Creating Goals

Kelly (2001) wrote that the first step in skill development is goal setting. In Lewis Carroll's book, *Alice in Wonderland* (1960), Alice asks the Cheshire cat, "'Would you tell me, please, which way I ought to go from here?' 'That depends a good deal on where you want to get to,' said the cat.' 'I don't much care where . . .' said Alice. 'Then it doesn't matter which way you go,' said the cat" (p. 64).

When approaching skill development, interpreters cannot be like Alice. When asked what areas need attention, an appropriate response is not "everything," or "I just want to get better." Skill development requires direction. Isham (1983) writes that self-directed growth for interpreters should include goal setting, time frames, written records, feedback, and guidance. Goals consist of a desired outcome of a behavior and communicate the will to improve (Gordon, 1999).

The more specific and measurable a goal is the better, because improvement can be more easily recognized. "I can't voice" is not as effective as, "I have problems with adding the word "and" to every sentence." Once a goal has been set, commitment to follow through can occur.

To determine areas of weakness, interpreters can record themselves interpreting both a dialogic and a monologic discourse. Areas that need improvement can become very apparent by putting the tape away for a couple of days, and then, either alone or with a mentor, listening to it without watching the source material. By listening only to the audiotape, the interpreter has only the target language, which is what an English consumer hears, without any benefit of the signed message.

Prioritizing Goals

After goals have been selected, they need to be prioritized (Isham, 1983). Everything cannot be fixed at once. If several problem areas have been identified, they should be written down in order of importance and thought about.

Practicing

Once the first goal has been selected, there is a need to practice. Practicing does not only mean looking at ASL and trying to convert it into an appropriate English interpretation. A lot of work is done on the mental level before a word is even uttered. One must think about the discourse to be produced, taking the time to reflect on the material and how it can best be interpreted. Listening to other interpreters and trying to understand why certain techniques are effective or ineffective can be helpful, as well as practicing a text more than once. Knowing what is coming is not cheating. The repetition helps interpreters master problem areas that will carry over into other situations. This helps interpreters gain competence and confidence in their skill.

Seeking a Mentor

It is advantageous to find someone to work with rather than trying to improve skills alone. When working with a mentor, pragmatic issues must be dealt with before skill development begins. Decisions need to be made concerning the length of the mentoring relationship and the goals. The South

Central Pennsylvania RID suggests that, "in order to avoid conflicts, expectations need to be clearly explained and understood by both the mentor(s) and the mentee before the program begins" (Breinich, 2001, p. 25). For example, the two parties might agree from the start to meet once a week for four weeks. At the end of the specified end time, there can be a mutual agreement to continue or stop.

Working interpreters who are not yet certified may want to look into the option of being paired with certified interpreters who can help them with their skills and help them decide when they are ready to take the certification exam. Many agencies are open to a request of certified interpreters to work with not-yet-certified interpreters for skill enhancement. This type of mentoring should not only include time on the job, but also pre-assignment planning and post-assignment feedback. Before beginning this type of mentorship, the mentor may want to listen to the mentee's ability to interpret into English.

There are ways mentees can maximize a mentoring relationship (Maxwell, 1995). Mentees need to be open to learning. They do not need to try to impress the mentor. Constantly trying to show how much one knows will set up a barrier to learning. Whatever is learned should be put into practice as soon as possible. Learn it; practice it; do it; keep it.

Working with Deaf Consumers

To be able to produce a coherent message, interpreters need to understand the topic of the presentation. When working with a Deaf presenter, Hodek and Radatz (1995) state that only when working in a partnership can an interpreter provide the highest quality interpreting services. This partnership consists of:

1. The Deaf presenter and interpreter seeing themselves as partners who have different roles, but the responsibility for success is shared.

2. The interpreter knowing what is needed in order to do his or her best work.

3. The presenter needing to understand his or her own presentation style.

4. The presenter needing to provide the interpreter with an outline, handouts, copies of overheads and other materials in advance so the interpreter can review and study them.

5. The interpreter and presenter meeting to discuss the outcomes the presenter is hoping to accomplish.

6. The interpreter and presenter discussing how the interpreter can signal a request for clarification and additional time to complete an interpretation, or how to manage interaction with the audience.

The interpreter must also realize that every consumer is different. What may work with one consumer may not work with another. Even if the interpreter is familiar with the topic, he or she should still look over the materials in order to have the vocabulary fresh, and think through how the presentation is to be made.

Summary

All the work and study that interpreters put into their job occurs in order to guide listeners to understand the message. To be able to do this, interpreters must look beyond the words, and focus on the whole text. Seleskovitch (1978) states it so eloquently when she writes:

> Conscious of the task he must perform, the interpreter constantly strives to have the listeners understand what the speaker says, and to do this he speaks to them personally to 'explain' to them what cannot be readily translated. Knowing that, he must transmit the meaning of what he himself has understood. In short, he cooperates with the listener to make sure he understands (p. 113).

When interpreting into English, an effective interpreter will strive for accuracy and preservation of meaning; and with an ASL-to-English interpretation, the interpreter will then be able to say it like they mean it.

Activity 10-1

Vocal tone

Step 1: Select an article, poem, or reading that contains emotional text. The text should be between one or two pages long.

Step 2: Practice reciting the piece out loud with appropriate emotion.

Step 3: Audiotape the piece.

Step 4: Play it back, noting what was effective and ineffective.

Were any of the following voice flaws apparent?

Breathiness	Whininess
Whispery quality	High pitch
Nasal twang	Screechy tone
Shrill tone	Monotone

Were any of the following voice qualities present?

Firmness	Strength
Low-pitch	Color
A soothing quality	Persuasiveness

Step 5: Record the piece again with modifications for improvement.

Optional Step: Ask another person to listen to the tape. Have him/her give feedback on vocal quality.

Was there a distinct beginning, middle, and end to all sentences?

What were the positive features about the presentation?

Was appropriate emotion was conveyed in the voice?

Did the listener have any problem understanding what was said?

Activity 10-2

In-class activity

Step 1:   Acquire a film that uses no language, such as a silent film or a cartoon without words.

Step 2:   Either alone or with a team, "interpret" into English the contents of the film. Record the interpretation on an audiotape.

Step 3:   Later, play the audiotape and listen to message. Answer the following questions.

  1.   Were the sentences complete?

  2.   Were there clean breaks when the subject changed?

  3.   Were word choices consistent?

  4.   Was the vocal tone appropriate?

  5.   Was all the information related clearly?

  6.   Was the spirit of each character conveyed clearly?

Activity 10-3

Comparing the baseline for progress

At the beginning of the class, each student made a recording of an ASL-to-English interpretation to establish a baseline. Using the same material, re-record an English interpretation. Later, review both audiotapes, noting differences between the two. Answer the following questions:

What word choices were different?

Were the English sentences more complete?

Was the English presented in a more idiomatic manner? How?

What was done effectively in the first interpretation?

What was not done effectively in the first interpretation?

What was done effectively in the second interpretation?

What was not done effectively in the second interpretation?

Students should look for completeness of sentences, word choice, English grammar, volume, tone, expression, handling of direct address, pronouns, spatial information, classifiers, topic/comment, and reading of fingerspelling and numbers.

Activity 10-4

Establishing interpreting goals

Step 1:   Audiotape a 10-minute ASL-to-English interpretation.

Step 2:   List all the consistent problem areas. These could include:

> Word choice
>
> Idiomatic phrasing
>
> Understanding of fingerspelling and numbers
>
> Completeness of sentences
>
> Use of language regulators
>
> Transition markers

Step 3:   Of the problems listed, choose two which are the most important to work on for skill development.

Step 4:   Listen to the audiotape and find examples of other problem areas that should be worked on. Describe each pattern in as much detail as possible.

Step 5:   For each area in which the process breaks down, list two concrete goals to work on to strengthen the interpretation.

Step 6:   Write these goals in a place where they can be referred to easily.

Step 7:   Work on skill improvement.

Bibliography

Aero, R., & Weiner, E. 1981. *The Mind Test*. New York, NY: William Morrow Publications.

Akamatsu, C.T., & Stewart, D.A. 1989. The role of fingerspelling in simultaneous communication, *Sign Language Studies*. 65:361-374. Silver Spring, MD: Linstok Press, Inc.

Bahleda, S.J. 1997. A positive approach to fingerspelling instruction, *Celebrating the Vision: RID in the 21st Century, Proceedings of the 15th National Convention of the Registry of Interpreters for the Deaf*. (pp. 25-29). Silver Spring, MD: Registry of Interpreters for the Deaf, Inc.

Baker, C. 1977. Regulators and turn-taking in American Sign Language discourse, in L. A. Friedman (ed.), *On the Other Hand: New Perspectives on American Sign Language*. (pp. 215-236). Dept. of Linguistics, University of California, Berkeley, California: Academic Press, Inc.

Baker-Shenk, C. 1991. The interpreter: machine, advocate, or ally? in J. Plant-Moeller (ed.), *Proceedings of the 12th National Convention of the Registry of Interpreters for the Deaf*. (pp. 120-140). Silver Spring, MD: Registry of Interpreters for the Deaf, Inc.

Barik, H.C. 1975. Simultaneous interpretation: qualitative and linguistic data, *Language and Speech*. 18:272-297. Middlesex, UK: Kingston Press, Ltd.

Bar-Tzur, D. 2001. Frozen Register and the Translation Process from English to ASL, hometown.aol.com/bartzur/index.html

Battison, R. 1978. *Lexical Borrowing in American Sign Language*. Silver Spring, MD: Linstok Press, Inc.

Barnwell, K. 1980. *Introduction to Semantics and Translation*. Horsleys Green, England: Summer Institute of Linguistics.

Beach, W.A. 1993. Transitional regularities for "casual" "okay" usages, *Journal of Pragmatics*. (pp. 325-352). New York, New YorK: Elsevier Science Publishers.

Beare, K. 2001. Register Use in English, English as 2nd Language, http://esl.about.com/library/weekly/aa091001chtm

Berlo, D. K. 1960. *The Process of Communication*. New York, NY: Holt, Rinehart and Winston, Inc.

Bragg, B. 1990. Communication and the Deaf community: Where do we go from here? in M.D. Garretson (ed.), *Communication Issues Among Deaf People - Eyes, Hands, and Voices: A Deaf American Monograph*. (pp. 9-14). Silver Spring, MD: National Association of the Deaf, Inc.

Breinich, R. 2001. SCPARID's mentorship program, *The Views*. 18:10.

Brislin, R.W. 1981. *Cross-Cultural Encounters: Face-to-Face Interaction*. New York, NY: Pergamon Press.

Carlson, R.H., & Morgan. S.M. 1980. Sign-to-voice interpreting, *A Century of Deaf Awareness in a Decade of Interpreting Awareness.* (pp. 144-156). Silver Spring, MD: Registry of Interpreters for the Deaf, Inc.

Carroll, L. 1960. *Alice's Adventures in Wonderland.* New York: Signet Classic Printing.

Carroll, L. 1986. *Through the Looking Glass and What Alice Found There.* New York, NY: Knopf Publishers.

Conference of Interpreter Trainers 1995. National Interpreter Education Standard, Approved.

Cokely, D. 1992. *Interpretation: A Sociolinguistic Model.* Silver Spring, MD: Linstok Press.

Cokely, D. 2001. Interpreting culturally rich realities: research implications for successful interpretations, *Journal of Interpretation, Millennial Edition.* (pp. 1-45). Silver Spring, MD: Registry of Interpreters for the Deaf, Inc.

Cokely, D., & Baker, C. 1980. *American Sign Language: A Student Text.* Silver Spring, MD: T.J. Publishers, Inc.

Colonomos, B.M. 1989. *The Interpreting Process: A Working Model.* Manuscript. Riverdale, MD: The Bicultural Center.

Davis, J. 1989. Distinguishing language contact phenomena in ASL interpretation, in C. Lucas (ed.), *The Sociolinguistics of the Deaf Community.* (pp. 85-102). San Diego, CA: Academic Press, Inc.

Dickerson, W.B. 1987. Orthography as a pronunciation resource, in A. Brown (ed.), *Teaching English Pronunciation: A Book of Readings.* (pp. 11-20). Routledge Publisher, London, New York.

Frishberg, N. 1990. *Interpreting: An Introduction.* Silver Spring, MD: Registry of Interpreters for the Deaf, Inc.

Frishberg, N. 1997. Working with silent films: separating translation from voicing skills, *Celebrating the Vision: RID in the 21st Century, Proceedings of the 15th National Convention of the Registry of Interpreters for the Deaf.* (pp. 51-57). Silver Spring, MD: Registry of Interpreters for the Deaf, Inc.

Friedman, L.A., Ed. 1977. *On the Other Hand: New Perspectives On American Sign Language.* New York, NY: Academic Press.

Fromkin, V., & Rodman, R. 1978. *An Introduction to Language.* New York, NY: Holt, Rinehart and Winston.

Gish, S. 1991. Ethics and decision making for interpreters, Telecourse Workbook. Western Oregon State College. Monmouth, OR

Gordon, J. R. 1999. *Organizational Behavior: A Diagnostic Approach.* Upper Saddle River, NJ: Prentice Hall.

Groode, J.L. 1992. *Fingerspelling: Expressive and Receptive Practice,* video. San Diego, CA: DawnSignPress, Inc.

Guillory, L.M., 1966. *Expressive and Receptive Fingerspelling for Hearing Adults.* Baton Rouge, LA: Claitor Publishing Division.

Halliday, M.A.K. 1968. The users and uses of language, in J. Fishman (ed.), *Readings in the Sociology of Language.* (pp. 139-169). The Hague: Mouton.

Halliday, M.A.K., & Hassan, R. 1978. *Language as a Social Semitoic.* Baltimore, MD: University Park Press.

Hodek, B., & Radatz, J. 1996. Deaf professionals and sign-to-voice interpretations: chaos or success?, *A Celebration of the Profession,* Proceedings of the Fourteenth National Convention of the Registry of *Interpreters for the Deaf, August 1-5, 1995.* (pp. 140-151). Silver Spring, MD: Registry of Interpreters for the Deaf, Inc.

Hodges, J. C., & Whitten, M.E. 1982. *Harbrace College Handbook.* New York, NY: Harcourt Brace Jovanovich, Inc.

Humphries, T., Padden, C., & O'Rourke, T.J. 1980. *A Basic Course in American Sign Language.* Silver Spring, MD: T. J. Publishers

Humphrey, J. 2000. Discourse Markers: The Glue of an Interpretation. Workshop presentation handouts. San Diego, CA.

Humphrey, J.H., & Alcorn, B.J. 1995. *So You Want To Be an Interpreter? An Introduction to Sign Language Interpreting.* Amarillo, TX: H & H Publishers.

Interpreter Education Center. 1997. *Language Use in ASL: Register,* video. Region X Interpreter Education Center, Western Oregon University. Monmouth, OR

Isham, B. 1983. Beyond the classroom: self-directed growth for interpreters, *The Reflector.* 6: 15-17.

Jacobsen, M. 2001. Linguistic Style Levels, handout. English 333 class at West Texas A & M University.

Jannedy, S. R., Poletto, T.L., & Weldon, T. 1994. Language Files: Materials for an Introduction to Language and Linguistics. Columbus, OH: Ohio State University Press.

Joos, M. 1968. The Isolation of Styles, in J. Rishman (ed.), *Readings in the Sociology of Language.* (pp. 185-191). The Haugue: Mouton.

Kannapell, B. 1982. Inside the Deaf community. *The Deaf American.* 34: (4): 23-26.

Kannapell, B, 1989. Inside the Deaf community, in Wilcox, S. (ed.), *American Deaf Culture: An Anthology.* (pp. 21-28). Silver Spring, MD: Linstok Press.

Kelly, J. 1998. What are we becoming? *The Views.* 15:8.

Kruger, J. & Dunning, D. 1999. Unskilled and unaware of it: how difficulties in recognizing one's own incompetence lead to inflated self-assessments, *Journal of Personality and Social Psychology.* (pp. 1121-1134). Cornell University, American Psychological Association.

Larson, M.L. 1998. *Meaning-Based Translation, A Guide To Cross-Language Equivalence.* Lanham, MD: University Press of American, Inc.

Lawrence, S. 1994. Interpreter discourse: English to ASL expansion, in E.A. Winston (ed.), *Proceedings of the 10th National Convention Conference of Interpreter Trainers.* (pp. 204-215). Charlotte, N.C.: Conference of Interpreter Trainers.

Marron, S. 1999. *Comparing ASL and English Features: Implications For Voice Interpreting,* video with booklet. Torrance, CA: Regional Interpreter Training Consortium.

Maxwell, J.C. 1995. *Developing the Leaders Around You.* Nashville, TN: Thomas Nelson Publishers.

McCawley, J. D. 1981. *Everything That Linguists Have Always Wanted to Know about Logic, but Were Ashamed to Ask.* Chicago, IL: University of Chicago Press.

McIntire, M. 1984. Task analysis—theory and application, *Conference of Interpreter Trainers Proceedings of the Fifth National Convention,* (pp. 29-69). Silver Spring, MD: Registry of Interpreters for the Deaf, Inc.

Mendoza, L. 1999. The ABC's of Fingerspelling, thesis. San Diego, CA: University of California.

Metzger, M. 1999. *Sign Language Interpreting: Deconstructing the Myth of Neutrality.* Washington, DC: Gallaudet University Press.

Miller, G. R. 1972. *An Introduction to Speech Communication.* New York, NY: Bobbs-Merrill.

Mindess, A. 1999. Reading between the signs: a practical approach to cultural adjustment, *Honoring Our Past, Creating Our Future Together: Proceedings of the 16th National convention of the Registry of Interpreters for the Deaf.* (pp. 141-168). Silver Spring, MD: Registry of Interpreters for the Deaf, Inc.

Monikowski, C. 1994. Issue III: Proficiency, in E. Winston, (ed.), Mapping our Course: A Collaborative Venture. *Proceedings of the Tenth National Convention, Conference of Interpreter Trainers*, 1994 CIT Proceedings. Conference of Interpreter Trainers.

Morris, W., Ed. 1980. *The American Heritage Dictionary of the English Language.* Boston, MA: Houghton, Mifflin Co.

Neumann-Solow, S. 1981. *Sign Language Interpreting: A Basic Resource Book.* Silver Spring, MD: National Association of the Deaf.

O'Connor, J. & Seymour, J. 1990. *Introducing Neuro Linguistic Programming: The New Psychology of Personal Excellence.* London: Hartnolls Limited.

Padden, C. 1991. The acquisition of fingerspelling by Deaf children, in P. Siple & S. Fischer (eds.), *Theoretical Issues in Sign Language Research, Psychology.* (pp. 191-210). Chicago: The University of Chicago Press.

Parker, F., & Riley, K. 1994. *Linguistics for Non-Linguists: A Primer with Exercises.* Boston, MA: Allyn and Bacon.

Patrie, C. 2000. *English Skills Development.* San Diego, CA: DawnSignPress.

Patrie, C. 1989. Fingerspelled word recognition and rapid serial visual processing in hearing adults: A study of novice and expert sign language interpreters. Ann Arbor, MI: U.M.I.: University of Maryland College Park Dissertation

Peterson, R. 2002. Metacognition and recall protocols, in C. Roy (ed.), *Innovative Practices for Teaching Sign Language Interpreters.* (pp. 132-15). Washington, DC: Gallaudet University Press.

Quigley, S.P. & Youngs, J.P. 1965. *Interpreting for Deaf People.* Washington, DC: U.S. Department of Health, Education and Welfare, Rehabilitation Services Administration.

RSA Federal Interpreting Center. 1995. (No. CSDA 84.160A). *Professional Development Endorsement System: A Curriculum for Training Interpreters for the Deaf in Educational and Rehabilitation Settings,* September, 1995. No. CSDA 84:160A. Winstead, CT: RSA

Roy, C. 1989. Features of discourse in an American Sign Language lecture, in C. Lucas (ed.), *The Sociolinguistics of the Deaf Community.* (pp. 231-251). Dept. of Linguistics, Gallaudet University, Washington, DC: Academic Press, Inc.

Roy, C. 1993. A sociolinguistic analysis of the interpreter's role in simultaneous talk in interpreted interaction, *Multilingual Journal of Cross-Cultural and Interlangauge Communication.* 12 (4): 341-363. Berlin: Mouton.

Sacks, H. 1984. *On Being Ordinary, Structures of Social Action Studies.* (pp 413-429). New York, NY: Cambridge University Press.

Sacks, H., Schegloff, E. & Jefferson, G. 1974. A simplest systematic for the organization of turn-taking in conversation, *Language.* 50(4): 696-735. Washington, DC: Linguistic Society of America.

Schegloff, E. A. 1980. Preliminaries to preliminaries: "Can I ask you a question?" *Sociological Inquiry.* 50:104-152. Arizona State University. Tempe, AZ

Schegloff, E. A. 1981. Discourse as an interactional achievement: some uses of "uh huh" and other things that come between sentences, in D. Tannen (ed.), *Analyzing Discourse, Text and Talk*. (pp. 71-93). Washington, DC: Georgetown University Roundtable on Languages and Linguistics.

Schein, E.H. 1992. *Organizational Culture and Leadership*. San Francisco, CA: Jossey-Bass Publishers.

Seleskovitch, D. 1978. *Interpreting for International Conferences: Problems of Language and Communication*. Washington, DC: Pen and Booth.

Shuey, E. 2001. Improving Interpretation: Your Formal English Skills, notes from a presentation at the RID National Conference, Orlando, FL.

Simon, J. H., & Maroney, E.M. 1997. Register: Theory and practice for interpreting educators, Celebrating the Vision: RID in the 21st Century, *Proceedings of the 15th National Convention of the Registry of Interpreters for the Deaf*. (pp. 103-112). Silver Spring, MD: Registry of Interpreters for the Deaf, Inc.

Skrebels, P. 1997. Language Notes, University of South Australia. Flexible Learning Centre, University of South Australia, www.i.roma.unisa.edu.au/07118/language/intro.htm

Smith, C., Lentz, E.M., & Mikos, K. 1988. *Signing Naturally: Level 1*. San Diego, CA: DawnSignPress, Inc.

Solow, S.N. 1981. *Sign Language interpreting: A Basic Resource Book*. Silver Spring, MD: National Association of the Deaf.

Spears, R.A. 1998. *Phrases and Idioms: A Practical Guide to American English Expressions*. Chicago, IL: NTC Publishing Group.

Spingarn, T.N. 2001. Knowledge of Deaf community-related words, symbols, and acronyms among hearing people: implications for the production of an equivalent interpretation, *Journal of Interpretation Millennial Edition*. (pp 69-84). Silver Spring, MD: Registry of Interpreters for the Deaf, Inc.

Sternberg, M.L.A. 1987. *American Sign Language Dictionary*. New York, NY: Harper & Row.

Stauffer, L.K. 1991. Enhancing visualization skills for interpreting between ASL and English, in J. Plant-Moeller (ed.), *Expanding Horizons Proceedings of the Twelfth National Convention of the Registry of Interpreters for the Deaf*. (pp 62-80). Silver Spring, MD: Registry of Interpreters for the Deaf, Inc. February 25, 2002. Milestones Section, *Time Magazine*. (p. 23).

Tipton, C. 1999. "Challenges to Voice Interpreting." Workshop handout.

Tipton, C. 2003. "To Quote Or Not To Quote: Direct Address For Interpreters." Workshop handout.

Vassallo, W. 1990. *Speaking with Confidence, A Guide for Public Speakers*. Crozet, VA: Betterway Publications, Inc.

Wells, J.M. 1983. Comprehension of fingerspelled words and numbers within signed messages: skill development strategies and exercises, *Proceedings of the 8th National Convention of the Registry of Interpreters for the Deaf: Golden Opportunities in Interpreting*. (pp. 147-160). Silver Spring, MD: Registry of Interpreters for the Deaf, Inc.

Waldhorn, A., & Zeiger, A. 1981. *English Made Simple*. Garden City, NY: Doubleday and Company.

Zimmer, J. 1989. Toward a description of register variation in American Sign Language, in C. Lucas, (ed.), *Sociolinguists of the Deaf Community*. (pp. 253-272). San Diego, CA: Academic Press.

Zimmer, J. 1991. Appropriateness and naturalness in ASL/English interpreting, in J. Plant-Moeller (ed.), *Expanding Horizons, Proceedings of the Twelfth National Convention of the Registry of Interpreters for the Deaf*. (pp. 81-92). Silver Spring, MD: Registry of Interpreters for the Deaf, Inc.